Come
TO
THE
Edge

Other Books by James L. (Jim) Killen, Jr.

God's New Possibility

Refinery, a Novel

The Message of Salvation

What Can We Believe?

Pastoral Care in Small Membership Churches

What Does The Lord Require?

Who Do You Say that I Am?

I Believe

Come TO THE Edge

An Invitation To Adventure

JIM KILLEN

iUniverse, Inc.
Bloomington

iUniverse books may be ordered through booksellers or by contacting:

iUniverse
1663 Liberty Drive
Bloomington, IN 47403
www.iuniverse.com
1-800-Authors (1-800-288-4677)

Because of the dynamic nature of the Internet, any web addresses or links contained in this book may have changed since publication and may no longer be valid. The views expressed in this work are solely those of the author and do not necessarily reflect the views of the publisher, and the publisher hereby disclaims any responsibility for them.

ISBN: 978-1-4759-7795-0 (sc)
ISBN: 978-1-4759-7796-7 (e)

Printed in the United States of America

iUniverse rev. date: 2/27/2013

To everyone whom I have ever loved and everyone who has ever loved me.

*R*eligion is getting a bad rap these days. Lots of people are deciding that they just don't need it. When I consider the amount of superstition and bigotry that is being practiced in the name of religion, I can understand how those people feel. But doing without religion really doesn't work. Every person, and also every community, has some set of basic beliefs and values and relationships that shape their lives. Those things are your religion, whether or not you choose to call it that. That being the case, it seems better to think through the things that are going to shape your life instead of just drifting into them. For the sake of those who choose to do that, I would like to share my reflections on religion and life in the hope that some of the big basic beliefs of the Christian Faith may come to make sense and to have value for those who choose to read.

The brief reflections I will share in this book appeared first in a blog that I wrote for a while. I am a retired pastor. For forty five years, I stood in a pulpit on most Sundays and shared the messages that came to me as I lived in the conversation between the biblical faith and life in today's world. After my retirement, I continued to live in that conversation and the messages kept coming but I had no place to share them. I chose to publish them in a blog for any who might care to read. If you read my book, you will soon see that I don't just believe what everyone else believes. I confess that there are some fresh insights that I am just busting to share. But I believe that I am staying close to the really big essentials of the Christian faith, perhaps closer that some of the more widely held traditions. And you will see that I will be relating them to the life you are living every day in the real world. I believe that is what it is all about.

I have chosen "Come to the Edge" as a title for my blog and for my book. You may recognize that this comes from a strange little poem that the poet Christopher Logue wrote in honor of the French poet and critic, Guillaume Appolinaire. I am surprised at how many places I find that poem being quoted. I suspect that the author didn't have anything especially religious in mind when he wrote it. But I find that it says something very significant about the Christian faith as I have experienced it. In the poem, a speaker keeps saying, "Come to the Edge." The responders keep resisting, saying, "No. It's too high. We might fall." Finally the speaker shouts "Come to the edge." And the poet says, "They came, and he pushed, and they flew."

I realize that, for many people, religion has always been a secure place into which to retreat from the stresses of life. For me, the Christian faith has always been something that is constantly calling me out of the familiar, the comfortable, the safe places in life and leading me to the frontiers of my understanding and experience where discoveries are made.

I decided to translate my blogs into a series of short readings, devotional readings if you choose to use them as such, when I learned that I have a melanoma that will probably limit the length of my remaining life. I chose to do this to put into some written form all of the things I have most wanted to share so that I could leave them with those whom I love. You will find occasional reflections on things that were going on in my personal life as I prepared to do my sharing. I hope that you will find them meaningful.

It would be impossible for me to give credit to all who have contributed to this book. As you will see, everyone whose life has ever touched mine has made a contribution. But I must say a special "Thank you" to my wife and partner, Juanita, who has helped me in the preparation of this manuscript in many ways.

I invite you to come to the edge with me and see what we may discover. I invite you to come with me on an adventure in faith.

Table of Contents

Finding the Way Into A Personal Relationship With God, Reflections on the Witness of Paul, Romans 8

Random Reflections on Some Really Big Questions

Discovering the Shape of Reality

Reflections on Big Ideas from the Hebrew Scriptures

Where Is God?

Where is God? That is a big question that we all need to answer. Lots of people answer quickly: "Of course, God is in heaven" or "God is in church" or "God is in all of the things we call religious." Those are the places where we go to get in touch with God. But the Bible gives another answer. The Bible tells us about a God who is present and at work in the world in which we live everyday—and in the working out of human history—and in our encounters with the realities of every day life. The scriptures and religious traditions tell us what others who have gone before us have learned about God through their encounters with God in life and history. It is important for us to pay attention to what they tell us so that we will be able to recognize God and to understand what God is doing when we meet God in our own lives. It is important for us to know how to recognize what God is doing and to respond in ways that will enable God's saving work to be done in us and through us.

Well, just how does that work? I think I can explain by sharing a personal witness. A few months ago, my doctor called to give me the results of some tests. He said: "Jim, you have a melanoma. You need to go the M. D. Anderson hospital in Houston and get it attended to." I know that some cynical people would want to say, "Okay Christian, where was your God when he let that happen to you?" There are lots of people who think that God is supposed to always make everything come out alright and good. When that doesn't happen, they think God is not there. But I have chosen to move into that experience looking to see God doing some of the same things the Bible writers have told us that God does.

The first thing I have experienced God doing in that situation is to remind me of my own limitedness and mortality. I am not God.

The doctor told me that I had an illness that I knew could kill me. I am just one more of the little creatures that come into being, lasts for a while, and then passes out of being—like the grass. Reminding us of our limitations is one of the things God does most often. Many people would not call that a saving experience but it is. That kind of awareness can help us to "gain a wise heart". (Psalm 90:12) That will enable us to remember who we are and stop taking the gift of being for granted. When we see how we fit into the scheme of things, we can live more realistically. We can remember to see and take in the color of the flowers and the way in which the sunset casts changing shadows on the bark of pine trees and all of the other beautiful things around us. By reminding me of my limitedness, God has enriched my life.

And one of the most beautiful things I have seen and experienced in this encounter with reality is love. I believe that all real love is an expression of God's love. When I think of all of the selfishness and hatred in the world, I know that love is not to be taken for granted. It does not just happen. It is something miraculous that God makes happen. (1 John 4:16) I have experienced a lot of love as I have gone through this difficult time. Members of my family, members of my church, members of my larger faith community, my neighbors, and especially one special person have loved me and cared what was happening to me and lifted me up in prayer. They have also done lots of practical loving things to be helpful to me. That is no little thing. It is not easy to love a guy who has cancer. That love is costly—like the love God gave to us through the suffering and death of Jesus. I have read about the love of God in the Bible. Now I have experienced it. It is a reality for me.

And I believe that I am experiencing God's healing. We remember that Jesus went around healing sick people. That is just one expression or the saving work of God about which the Bible says so much. God gives being and wholeness in situations in which they could easily be lost. That is one of the most important themes in the whole witness of the Bible. All healing is miraculous. Yes, I am being cared for in an awesome institution in which sophisticated doctors apply skills learned from the most advanced scientific research. But, where did we get the idea that science and religion are in conflict. God is working through that hospital in just the same way in which he worked through the laying on of the hands of Jesus. All healing is miraculous. I believe that God is working for my healing.

It is important to remember that God's healing is intended to bring us to a wholeness that is bigger than just the healing of our physical bodies. Sometimes that wholeness comes even when physical healing can't—and it is the greater gift.

But what if I am not healed? I have no guarantee. I am no more deserving of healing than many others who have not been healed. And at my age, as I watch the rest of my life go flitting by at an ever accelerating rate, I know that it cannot be long before something will bring my life to an end. Then where will God be? I hope that, when I come to that time, I will remember that I have experienced the reality of God—and of God's love—and of God working to give being even where being is in jeopardy. I hope that I can remember that the God who has loved me and given me being is not someone who is limited as I am. God must be someone who is eternal. That same God who has loved me and given me being throughout my life must be there beyond my death. I hope that I will be able to remember that I have experienced the reality of God and go to meet my death in courage, trusting God to be there.

There is a story in the Bible in which the question, "Where is God?" takes on a special meaning. It is the story of the beginning of the ministry of the prophet Elisha. (2 Kings 2:9-15) Elisha had followed his mentor, Elijah, the greatest prophet the people of Israel had ever known. Knowing that Elijah would soon be taken from him, Elisha followed him on a journey that took them across the Jordan River. As Elijah was being taken up to God, his mantel fell off. Elisha picked the mantel up and then went back to the Jordan River, intending to cross it and take up the work that Elijah had done. He knew he could not do that work alone. He would have to do it trusting in God. So he took the mantel of Elijah and said, "Where is the God of Elijah?", and he struck the water of the river with the mantel. The river parted and let him cross. When we have to venture out into new situations in life in which we need to know that God is there—or into our death—we will be wise to remember what we have experienced of the reality of God and say,

"Where is the God of whom the biblical witnesses spoke?" and venture out trusting God to be there.

Prayer: Where are you God?

Let me add as a postscript a thought that often comes to me when I think of the question, "Where is God?" One summer, I spent a couple of months living and working on the Island of Utilla, off the coast of Honduras. I spent my first few days eagerly exploring my new and fascinating environment. The mission house where I lived was right on the shores of the Caribbean .In the mornings, I was awakened to the sound of gentle waves lapping against the shore. But when I looked out to sea, I could see nothing but the sea. I assumed that we were out of sight of the mainland. Then one especially clear morning, I looked out to sea and saw the mountains of the mainland. They were beautiful. Of course, they had been there all of the time but some low hanging clouds has hidden them from me. Like the mountains of the mainland, the reality of God and of all that is eternal is always there and we live our lives in relationship with it even though we sometimes cannot see it.

Wrestling Angels

There is a story in the Hebrew Scriptures that has taken on special meaning for me. It is the story of Jacob wrestling with the angel. (Genesis 32:22-31) Jacob was a very "assertive" person and his assertiveness had led him into one conflict after another. The story took place at the time of a very important transition, a crisis, in his life. He was on a journey. He was camping out alone at night. The text says "a man wrestled with him until daybreak." Was he having a dream? Was he lying awake being tormented by the burdens of his past and his anxieties about his future? Or did someone actually come and wrestle with him? Tradition says it was an angel. Looking back on the experience, Jacob said it was God. Whatever it was that happened, it changed Jacob's life. He came away from the experience injured but blessed. He had a new vision—and a new way of relating to life—and a new name, Israel.

When philosophers write their learned books, they often devote one of the earliest chapters to explaining their "philosophical method", that is, to explaining how they intend to go about developing the rest of their system of thought. My philosophical method is one that I call, "wrestling angels."

Angels are messengers from God. There are lots of different kinds of angels. The great themes in the Bible and in Christian tradition are certainly messengers from God. Through them, the faithful adventurers from the past have witnessed to the discoveries they have made in their own experiences with God. Those witnesses have been passed on to us in the hope that they may lead us into our own interactions with God. Important experiences in our own lives can be messengers from God, especially those experiences that can make a difference in our lives. And some people, sometimes the most unlikely people, can play the role of angels. There must surely be other kinds of angels. God is not limited in the ways in which God can work in our lives.

My "philosophical method" is to try to recognize the messengers from God when they come into my life, to pay attention to them, to take them seriously, and to experience them in depth. I take hold of them—or let them take hold of me—and say to them: "Alright, what are you trying to show me?" Sometimes I don't like the answers I get—at least not at first. I sometimes come away from those encounters injured. But I often come away from them blessed.

When I try to put my discoveries together into an understanding of the meaning of life, I often find that I have insights that are in conflict or in tension with one another. I don't always feel that I must resolve those conflicts. I know that conflicts often occur when two or more significant insights are each showing me the limitations of the others. And I know that they may be showing me aspects of the tensions that keep life dynamic and growing. Sometimes some great doctrine of the church or some significant experience in life may not immediately bless me. Instead, it may leave me wondering, "What in the world was that all about?" When that happens, I do not feel that I have to discredit or discard it. I just let it stand there. Perhaps, when I visit it again, I will have lived my way into a place where I can understand what it is trying to show me.My discoveries do not always come together into nice neat systems of belief with no contradictions and with an answer for every question. Why should I expect my belief systems to take that shape. The Bible itself doesn't. That is not what it is all about. But they do often lead me into life shaping interactions with the living God. That *is* what it is about.

John and Charles Wesley, the nineteenth century churchmen who got the Methodist movement going, must have had lots of experience with wrestling angels. One of their favorite hymns was called: "Come O thou traveler unknown" or, simply, "Wrestling Jacob". It describes a religious experience, probably their own experience, in terms of wrestling with an angel. The song ends celebrating a life shaping discovery about the one who engaged them in so many of their life experiences. "The morning breaks, the shadows flee, pure universal love thou art. To me to all thy mercies move, thy nature and thy name is love." I suppose that no one can make that discovery—that is, really make it--except through wrestling with God. But those who do make it are profoundly blessed.

Prayer: Who are you, God, and who am I?

Riding the waves at

Galveston beach. Some lift me.

Some push me under.

God Creates

I often read again the story of the creation from the first chapter of the Bible. When I read that story, I often find myself being caught up in awe at the vastness of the universe as we now know it and in the intricacies of the life of the world around me. It always moves me to wonder. I can believe that all of this happened by evolution or by the other wondrous processes that the scientists are discovering—but I cannot believe that it happened by accident.

But, as wondrous as those first images are, the real climax of the story comes later in the chapter, when God creates humankind—you and me—in the image of God—to have dominion. That really is the point of the story. We will do well to save some of our wonderment for wondering what that means.

What does it mean that we are created in the image of God? There are other parts of the Bible that tell us we had better remember that God is God and we are not. And yet, we are created to be like God in some ways. That is an awesome—and frightening—thought.

What is God like? There is no way that our limited little minds can contain the reality of God. To talk about God at all, we have to talk in terms of metaphors, comparing God to ourselves so that we can compare ourselves to God. The story of creation does give us some helpful ways of thinking about God. It gives us the impression that God is one who knows, and understands, and acts intentionally. It tells us that God's acts have results. They make things happen. God acts freely and does what God chooses to do. God understands that things have meaning—and God gives meaning to things. If we read the many other chapters of the big book that starts with the creation story, we will discover that God continues to be creatively involved in the life and history of all that is created. And the story goes on to tell us that God does everything that God does in love. The love of God is something much bigger than what we are accustomed to calling love. (We will eventually get around to exploring that in depth.) We are led to believe that the act of creation was—is—an act of a love so great that it could not be self contained. It had to overflow in creativity, calling others into existence, others created in the image of God.

In what ways can we be like God? In many wonderful and frightening ways. We are like God in that we are endowed with the ability to know—and to understand—and to act intentionally. We are given the ability to act freely. That is an awesome thing. In spite of all of our talk about wanting freedom, we are really reticent to accept it and to act on it, especially when we realize the responsibility that comes with it. We actually spend a lot of our energy trying to get rid of freedom. And we can understand, if we will, that things have meaning and that some things are good and some things are bad. All of these are ways in which we are like God—whether we want to be or not. That is part of what it means to be human.

And, apparently, the rest of reality has been organized, to some extent, around our humanity. Our decisions and our actions do make things happen. Think of all of the good things and the bad things that humanity has made to happen. Think of the cures for diseases we have developed—and think of the ways in which human greed has reduced many to poverty. Think of the cities we have built—and think of the wars we have waged to destroy them.

Think of the things that you have made to happen. The frightening possibility that we can make things happen has been built into the order of creation. I suppose that is what it means that we are given "dominion." (Genesis 1:26) Apparently, we were created to participate with God in shaping the ongoing course of human life and history. That is scary, isn't it?

These are all ways in which we are already like God, whether we want to be or not. But there is another way in which we can be like God. It is a way that will have to be chosen and learned and practiced in sometimes costly ways. We can be like God in love. The rest of the story tells us that we are created to love like God loves and to participate with God in the loving things God is doing to shape human life and history. That love can only be entered into by way of a freely chosen commitment. And even after we have chosen it, it will not be easy to learn it or to practice it. But when we realize that our decisions and actions actually do help to shape the course of human life and history, then we must realize that both we and the rest of the creation have an urgent need for us to learn to love as God loves.

Prayer. This is scary, Lord. I hope I can live up to it.

Relationships Are Important

Relationships are important. They shape our lives. And through them, we are able to participate in shaping the lives of others and of the world.

More than fifty years ago, another person came into my life. We soon came into a relationship that we knew could be very important. We entered into a covenant with each other. Promises were made, promises that we would both have to grow up into. Commitments were made, commitments to trust and to be there to be trusted. We became partners in the adventure of life. We were there for each other through good times and bad times. My needs made demands on her. Her needs made demands on me. We each responded to the needs sometimes imperfectly, but the best we could.

That relationship, both the gifts and the requirements of it, did more than any other thing to shape my life. I believe that she would have said the same. And together we created a relational environment in which two other very fine people began to grow. I believe that our lives, both our lives together and the individual lives that were enabled by our togetherness, made some difference in the lives of some others and maybe in the world.

We lived out our covenant to love and to cherish, for better or for worse, for forty nine years until we were parted by death. And now, several years later, I have entered into a similar relationship with another person. I believe that such a relationship is a good example of what a covenant can be.

As important as that relationship is, there is another relationship that is even larger. It is bigger. It is not bigger because it competes with other relationships. It is bigger because it includes all other relationships.

I have just come from a hospital where I visited a young mother who was cradling a little baby girl, just twenty-four hours old. She rested in her mother's arms and looked around, blinking at the whole new world that was coming into focus around her. Eventually, her world will include mother and father and sisters and other people and houses and trees and birds and joys and sorrows and love and—yes hate, that has to be a part of it—and all of the things that love and hate produce. All of these things and others will be parts of the world as she will eventually experience it. Eventually, that reality will come together and form one whole. She will find herself living in relationship with one great other that is always there. Eventually, she will have to make some discoveries—and some decisions—about how that greater reality relates to her and how she will relate to it. That process of discovering and deciding and relating will go on throughout her life.

Within exactly that process of discovering and deciding and relating, the community of faith of which I am a part has made some bold—maybe audacious—discoveries—or decisions. We have decided to believe that the greater reality that/who is always there it is a reality that/who can meaningfully be thought of as being like a person. But of course none of our categories are adequate to contain that other. That other is the one who created everything that is and gives it to us. That other is there interacting with us in all of our interactions with life. That other is God.

Further, we have dared to believe that the great other who is God loves us and invites us to live in a covenant with it/him/her that is not unlike a marriage covenant, a relationship of mutual trust and love, a relationship in which there are both promises and expectations. (I hope you will forgive me for using masculine gender pronouns when I am talking about God. I know God is as feminine as she/he is masculine. But it is just too complicated to do anything else.)

This belief that God calls us to live in a covenant relationship with him runs through the whole Bible. It is the theme that ties the whole thing together, God made a covenant with the whole creation through Noah, (Genesis 9:8-17), and with a representative people through

Abram (Genesis 12:1-3) and again through Moses, (Exodus 19 and 20). And God reached out to invite us all into covenant through Jesus who is the Christ.

Do we dare to believe that the great other who meets us in all of life actually invites us to live our lives in a covenant of mutual love and trust with him? That would mean entering into all of our interactions with life in basic trust and love. It would mean entering into life believing that, in spite of all the things that are painful in life, there are certain promises and expectations that we can depend upon—and that we should make. Living in that kind of a covenant would certainly shape our lives. It might make of us agents for making a difference in the lives of others and of the world. We might even wonder, could it make a difference in that great other who is God?

Prayer: Hello, God. I am looking forward to getting acquainted with you.

The Possibility of Chaos

It is always a mistake to talk about love as if there is no hate and about good as if there is no evil. All you have to do is look around and you will discover that we are up against some things in life that can really mess things up if we let them. The Hebrew Scriptures are very realistic in this regard. There is a concept that is implied in many passages of scriptures that sums up the Old Testament's understanding of evil. It is the concept of chaos. Chaos represents confusion, destructive disorder, darkness, violence, and death. In the minds of the ancients, nothing represented chaos quite so well as the awful, turbulent depths of a stormy sea. Before God acted to create, everything was chaos. "In the beginning, when God created the heavens and the earth, the earth was formless and void and darkness covered the face of the deep, while a wind from God swept over the face of the waters." (Genesis 1:1-2 NRSV)

In the work of creation, God acted to bring order out of chaos, light out of darkness, being out of non-being, and life out of death. Modern scientists tell us that all of the apparently solid and substantial things we see around us are made of little bits of energy existing in delicately balanced relationships with one another. And if that order is broken, there is chaos—as in Hiroshima. Of course the Bible writers didn't know anything about that. But I am fascinated by the similarity between that discovery and the idea that God created everything by bringing order out of chaos.

God's creative work is not confined just to the physical world. God also does creative work in the social and personal aspects of reality as well, in the relationships between people—and groups—and nations. God works to bring order out of chaos and to move human society toward healthy social order in which the well being of all people is served. There is in the Hebrew Scriptures a concept of shalom, peace, which represents a kind of order within a person's life that makes possible wholeness and humanity. It is that kind of wholeness and well being that biblical people wished each other when they greeted each other with the words, "Peace be with you", "Shalom"

Now we ought to notice that, in none of these cases is being or wholeness or peace an inert or static thing. They all represent an order in which different forces exist in relationships and interactions with each other that are creative rather than destructive. If you want to see how that works, look at what is going on in your family when things are going well. Isn't it a situation in which different forces are working in healthy interactions with each other? A situation in which one force achieves order by forcing all of the others into submission is really not order. It is a conflict on the way to happening.

It should be obvious that in this, as in all of the works of God, God calls us to work with him and to participate in the work of bringing order out of chaos.

So, creation happens when God brings order out of chaos. And creation continues to happen as God works with and through us to maintain a creative relationship between the forces at work in the world. But here is something that is important to remember. When God creates, the chaos does not cease to exist. It is simply pushed back and held at bay, like the sea is held at bay by the dikes in the Netherlands. It is always waiting there ready to rush back in and destroy everything if the creative work ceases to hold it at bay. It is that kind resurgence of chaos that is represented by the story of the flood in the book of Genesis, (chapters 6-9). Remember, the book says that the flood was allowed to happen because…"the earth was corrupt in God's sight and the earth was filled with violence." (Genesis 6:11)

Peace, Shalom, represents human life put together in such a way that wholeness and humanity are possible. But look around and count the ways in which a life can disintegrate. We have the responsibility to find our way into a relationship with God, that great other reality, that will put our lives into a healthy order.

Look at the world in which we live. Is it not full of corruption and

17

violence and other destructive forces? We all remember that September day a few years ago when some people who had made hate into a religion flew airplanes full of people into the twin towers of the World Trade Center and into the Pentagon, and would have flown one into the nation's capital. Thousands of people were killed. Hate can be a terribly destructive thing. But not all of the hate is somewhere else. Harry Sarazin, a retired special agent for the F.B.I. tells us that there are 932 hate groups working in our own country today, (2011), a 50% increase since 2000. If we listen to the conversations going on around us, we can often hear hate expressing itself in the things that are said. And indifference may be even more destructive than hate. Being indifferent to the needs of those who are desperately poor can generate destructive hate. A nuclear holocaust is still something that could happen to our world. Yes, there are lots of bad things working in our world—and maybe in our lives—and they can do us harm. Behind every good and beautiful thing, there still lurks the possibility of chaos.

But God is at work in our world to hold chaos at bay and to bring being out of non-being, light out of darkness, wholeness out of sickness, life out of death and peace out of conflict. It is very important for us to know where that creative—saving—work is being done and to answer God's call to participate in it

Prayer: Lord, keep us afraid of the things we should be afraid of.

The Meaning of Salvation

What does it mean to be saved? That is an important question. But we don't think about it much. We think we already know the answer. To be saved means to have our guilt taken away so we can go to heaven after we die. That is what most of us think of when we think of salvation. But the Bible actually teaches a different understanding of salvation, a bigger understanding.

The Old Testament talks a lot about God being the savior. But it says little or nothing about going to heaven after we die. The Hebrew Scriptures tell about a God who is at work to save in this life and in human history. They tell about God saving people from things that oppress and threaten us in this life. They tell about God saving people to something better that God wants for us in this life. The great pivotal saving work of God of which the Old Testament tells is the exodus, that time when God saved the Hebrew people from slavery in Egypt and made them a nation in the Promised Land. To this day, Jewish people remember that saving work in their annual celebration of the Passover. To them, that is what it means to be saved.

The memory of the saving works God has done in the past teach us that there is a God who saves. They teach us to expect God to do saving works in our present and in our future. When the Hebrew people were defeated and taken away into exile in Babylon, the Hebrew prophets told the people to remember the saving works God did in the past and to expect God to act to save them again. Some of the Psalms retell the stories of God's saving works and call the people to remember and give thanks. "O give thanks to the Lord for he is good for his steadfast love endures forever." (Psalm 136) About half of the Psalms can be classified as laments or as penitential psalm (Psalm 3, Psalm 22, and Psalm 51 are

19

examples). They can be thought of as prayers for salvation. The psalmists lift their troubles up to God. They remember God's saving work in the past. And they ask God to save them from their present distress.

In all of these biblical teachings, God is thought of as one who works in our lives and in our world. God interacts with us and to save us from things that are bad for us in this life and to move us toward that better life that God wants for us here and now. Lots of people think that living a good life is a prerequisite for salvation, something you have to do to earn the right to go to heaven after you die. Actually, the good life is itself the prize, not the prerequisite. It is the good gift that God wants to give us. Rather late in the development of the faith of the Hebrew people, the people learned to expect that the God who is at work to save us in this life will also be at work to save us beyond this life as well.

The New Testament starts with this understanding of salvation. It tells us that God performed another great saving work in human history. God sent Jesus to make God known and to show us how God works in our lives and in our world to save us. We are taught to remember all of the ways in which God worked to save through Jesus –all of the ways. There are more than we usually remember. Then, when we see those same happening in our lives and in our world, we can recognize that God is at work there to save. Then we can respond in ways that will allow God's saving work to be done in us and through us.

Yes, the new and better life to which God wants to save us includes a hope that reaches beyond this life. But salvation is something that happens in this life. In the New Testament the Greek words that are usually translated, "to be saved" do not mean "to go to heaven". They mean "to be made whole".

I hope that you find this understanding of salvation exciting. It means that God's saving work relates to all of your deepest needs, not just to your guilt. And it means that salvation promises a new and better life here and now as well as here-after. We will explore that understanding of the saving work of God more fully in later reflections.

Prayer: Lord, help me to see what you are doing and to get excited about it.

Trusting the Invisible

The books of Exodus, Leviticus, Numbers and Deuteronomy in the Bible tell a very dramatic story. In that story, God sent Moses to lead the people of Israel out of slavery in Egypt and to take them on a long and torturous journey through a hostile wilderness and into a land where they could settle and become an important nation. From the "God side" of the story, God reached out to his people in love to save them and to move them toward the fulfillment of their God given destiny. God was reaching out to save his people. From the human side, this is a story of people leaving security and venturing out on a dangerous journey trusting the invisible God. It took great courage.

This was by no means a little or easy thing to do. In Egypt, the people were slaves. But they at least knew who they were and what was expected of them. They had to work hard and suffer abuse, but they had houses to live in and food to eat. They had security. When Moses came bringing a call from the God of a religious tradition that most of them could hardly remember, they were not immediately responsive. It took some rather spectacular occurrences to get the people ready to follow Moses.

Even after they did embark, they did not always follow faithfully. There were many crisis situations and in every crisis, there were people who wanted to go back to Egypt where they at least had food. Even while God was meeting Moses on a mountain top and renewing his covenant with them, they got impatient and made a rebellious return to paganism. Once when they were on the verge of completing their journey, they had a failure of trust that caused them to have to spend more time wandering in the wilderness and that kept most of them from being able to enter the Promised Land. It was a torturous journey. But in the process the people of Israel learned to live trusting the invisible God.

That is an important lesson for any person or nation to learn. When faced by the threats and uncertainties of life, we all have a temptation to hold on to the tangible things and to find security in the familiar things on which we have learned to depend. But every really significant endeavor will require us to let go of the familiar and to venture out of security and move out trusting the invisible. For the brave, this can become a way of life. It is called faith. That is another big lesson we can learn from the Hebrew Scriptures.

I once encountered a work of art that hovers in my memory as a symbol of that kind of faith. It is a faceted glass window that once adorned the youth center in the United Methodist Church in Seabrook Texas. A picture of the window is on the cover of this book. There is a story behind it.

Seabrook is located neat the Johnson Space Center through much of Americas adventure into space was planned and carried out. Several of the earliest astronauts, as well as many of the other space scientists were members of that church. For many of those earliest astronauts, the adventure into space was indeed an adventure in faith. Many of them were deeply religious. One astronaut actually got his mission named "Faith Seven".

One of the astronauts who was active in the church was Ed White. He and his family were faithful participants in the life of the church. He was one of the counselors in the youth program. Ed White was chosen to be the first American astronaut to step out of the space craft and "walk in space." Sadly, he was also one of the first astronauts to die in the service of the program. He and two other astronauts were killed in an explosion that took place on the ground as a result of a malfunction of some of the equipment. The whole country was in grief. The grateful community raised money for a significant memorial. They built a youth center on church property to serve the youth of the whole community.

A local artist, David Fosdick, designed a window for the front of the youth center to commemorate the astronauts. The window depicts Ed White in his space suit, floating outside of his space craft, tethered to it only by a fragile "umbilical cord" with both the earth and the moon in the distance. That image will always represent to me what it means to live by faith.

Prayer: Teach me to live trusting the invisible.

(Unfortunately both the church and the youth center were so badly damaged by a hurricane that the church had to relocate. The window is now in storage until a place can be found for it in a future building. I am grateful to David Fosdick, the artist, for allowing me to use the design for the Ed Whit window on the cover of this book.)

The Origin of Compassion

I want to tell you a story about how a friend of mine helped me to discover one of the really important connections within the Christian faith. It is the connection between being saved by God's grace and living a compassionate life.

My friend's name was Manuel. (It really was.) He was a man of the Jewish faith. Everyone joked about Manuel being the richest Jew in the small town where we lived. He and his family were the only Jews. But everyone also knew that Manuel was the most compassionate man in town. No needy person was ever turned away from Manuel's door.

I had a chance to see Manuel's compassion at work in a special way. Some of us, who were concerned about the amount of poverty in our county, became aware that the little poor children who did not have lunch money were being made to go into the school lunch room and watch the other children eat. Manuel said that he would go to the other business men in town and take up a collection for lunch money for the poor children if he could find some Christian to go with him. I went. The people of the community were not famous for their compassion for the poor. But, I heard Manuel say to one tough business man after another: "Have you ever been hungry? I've been hungry. I don't want those little children to go hungry. Their poverty is not their fault." The business men gave. The children ate.

Some time later, Manuel invited my family to visit his family during Passover to learn about their customs. He gave me a copy of the ritual that Jewish families used during those celebrations. I read how the Jewish people remember the saving work through which God saved the Jewish people from slavery in Egypt. I realized that the story must have had even more meaning for Manuel than it did for most Jews. Manuel was a survivor of the holocaust. He had grown up in Europe and he was there when Nazism spread its power over his country. Manuel was arrested with many others and put on one of those cattle trains that would take him to a death camp. Somehow Manuel escaped and made his way to a port in Belgium where he caught the last ship leaving for America. He knew that he had been saved. I began to realize that Manuel's experience of having been saved from the holocaust and the Jewish experience of being part of a people who have been saved, must be like the experience that Christians know as being saved by the grace of God. Being saved is not just a matter of believing that you have reservations in the her after. It is a matter of knowing that you have a life that is much better than the life that you might have had and knowing that you have not gotten it by pulling yourself up by your own boot straps. It is a gift from God.

As I read the story of the Exodus from the Passover ritual, I remembered another passage from the Hebrew Scriptures. Actually, there are several such passages. They come from the book of Deuteronomy in which Moses instructed the people who were on their way out of slavery in Egypt. He told them the ways in which they were to live in their promised land. These passages warn the people not to abuse the marginalized people among them, the widows and orphans and aliens, not to deal with them unjustly and not to be negligent of their needs. They were given a reason. "Remember that you were a slave in Egypt and the Lord your God redeemed you from there; therefore I command you to do this. (Deuteronomy 24:17-22)

There must be something about knowing that you have been saved from suffering and oppression and death that generates a sympathy for those who are still experiencing suffering and oppression and the threat of death. Remembering that we were saved by a power greater than ourselves must make us want to do what we can for others who are in need.

Can you see how a Christian's experience of having been saved by God's grace must be like the experience of a Jew, who knows that his people were saved from slavery or the experience of a man who was saved from the death camp? Being saved is a matter of knowing that we have life and love and meaning and hope and every other really important thing as a freely given gift from God who loves us. If we know ourselves saved in that way, we will have compassion for all who are in need. I suppose that we might measure the depth of our own experience of having been saved by the depth of our compassion for those who are in need.

Prayer: Lord, help me to see things as they really are and to learn both gratitude and compassion.

What Does The Lord Require?

If a nation will love the Lord God and walk in his ways, and obey his commandments, decrees, and ordinances, that nation shall live. But if they turn away, the nation will perish. (Paraphrased from Deuteronomy 30:15-20) That is a summary of one of the major themes of the Bible. It is the dominant theme of the book of Deuteronomy, the books of Deuteronomic history, and the books of the prophets. That is about half of the Old Testament. When any theme is that important, people who take the Bible seriously should pay attention to it. But what are twenty first century Americans to do with this theme?

There are some who believe that we should set aside the American tradition of separation of church and state and make our country a Christian country in some way that is similar to the way in which Saudi Arabia is a Muslim Country. There are some who think there would be some magic in doing symbolic things, like putting prayer back into public schools and hanging copies of the Ten Commandments on courthouse walls, that would win God's blessings for us. But most of us think those things would not solve our problems.

America has a tradition of religious pluralism in which a variety of religious orientations are accepted and appreciated. That is actually the religious heritage out of which American Democracy emerged. This is the heritage that most American citizens think can and should shape our public life today.

A heritage of pluralism, in which the government makes no laws to establish one religion or another as the religion of the nation, is different from a system of secularism, in which all religion is regarded as irrelevant. There should be a place for the secularist in this mix of traditions but there is no reason to think that we should establish secularism as the religion of the land. It seems that there is a danger that we could be doing just that. A vital pluralism is hard work. It requires us to work at understanding and appreciating the faiths of others. It invites people of all religious faiths to make their best contributions to the formation of life in the nation. But it cannot allow any one group to be able to "trump" the contributions of others.

At first it may seem that it might be difficult for a pluralistic country to live by the requirements of the book of Deuteronomy. But we have recently seen our country and others stumble into harms way by neglecting some religious teachings that are shared by most serious practitioners of most of the religions that make up our mix.

We have seen the world's economy crater to the disadvantage of almost everyone because of a lack of integrity in the management of the world's banking systems.

We have seen the ecosystems on which human life depends threatened by short sighted exploitation.

We have seen large parts of the world's population pushed into—or toward—poverty by the greed of the very wealthy and powerful. That poverty can generate frustration and frustration can turn into anger and anger can turn into hatred in all sorts of destructive ways—like terrorism.

We have seen classes and races and nations constantly competing against each other to gain their own advantage to the disadvantage of others. It is from such competition that international tensions and wars develop.

These things can indeed bring a nation down.

There are religious traditions that even a pluralistic nation—or world—can embrace that would make a difference in these things. A sense of being accountable to some higher power, who requires more of us than just an impressive end-of-year profit, could restore the integrity that would make the world's financial systems work again. A sense of responsible stewardship of the natural world could rescue the world from ecological disaster. A commitment to justice that will not allow the abuse or neglect of even the least of us could defuse the smoldering hatred that threatens us. And, if races and nations could learn to work together for the well being of all people instead of just competing for their own advantage then wars might finally cease on the face of the earth. All of these ways of living and relating are parts of what it means to live in love.

These are ideals to which most people already pay lip service. But to actually put them into practice will require a conversion of our nation and of others as well. No, it will not be enough just to hang the Ten Commandments on the courthouse walls. The change must be far reaching and demanding. But it is necessary. Americans cannot count on always being the most economically and militarily powerful nation in the world. We must learn instead to "...do justice, and to love kindness and to walk humbly with our God." (Micah 6:8)

Prayer: God, bless America—really—and all of the other countries too.

Choose Life

I think this would be a good time to share some reflections on my favorite verse of scripture to take out of context. Ordinarily, I think that interpreters should give a priority to the meaning that a lesson had to its original speaker or writer in its original context. But sometimes a verse can take on such special meaning in your own life that it can be regarded as a word from God to you. For me, one of those verses is made up of the two short words, "Choose life." These words come from a sermon that Moses preached to the people of Israel before they went into the Promised Land. He was urging them to be faithful to their covenant with the living God and not to allow themselves to be led astray by the attractive prosperity cults of the Canaanites. He said "I call heaven and earth to witness against you today that I have set before you life and death, blessing and curses. Choose life…". (Deuteronomy 30:19) It is easy to see what those words, "Choose life" meant in that context. But I think they can have an even bigger meaning that applies to every moment of life.

Life is given to us as a gift from God. But it has to be chosen before it can actually be all that God intends for it to be for us. A person has to say "yes" to life, to receive it, and to give himself or herself to living it as well as it can be lived. That is what it means to choose life.

There are those who do not choose life. A few weeks ago, a young person whom we all loved chose to end his own life. No one knows what made him stop being able to choose life. Some people choose ways of life that are counterproductive to life in its fullness. Don't think just of the drunkard or the drug addicts. There are people who choose very respectable, some might even say admirable, ways of trashing out their lives. That is what Moses was talking about. But some just fail to realize what is at stake in the ways in which they relate to life. Some take life for granted. Some act as if they think life is an imposition that they have to endure. Some live as if they are mad at the world. Some just forget to be grateful.

As you know, I am writing this while coping with an illness that will probably eventually end my life—if something else doesn't get me first. But I am choosing to do whatever I can to hold on to life. I have just gone through a treatment that I knew could be terribly expensive and cause lots of misery in the hope that it could prolong my life. It wasn't as bad as it might have been—or as successful. But I would not have thought of not trying it. I will try anything else that seems likely to prolong my life. For me, that is part of choosing life, but only part of it.

I suppose I have almost always chosen to choose life. For me, every day is Christmas and under the tree for me is the gift from God of another day of life. That really is something quite miraculous. I can't imagine how some people fail to see that. There is nothing more precious. I choose to receive that gift with great gratitude and celebrate it. That is true of the days of sadness and trouble as well as "the good days". They are all parts of the patchwork that makes up the beautiful tapestry of life. I will make the most of every day. I will enjoy all that is there to be enjoyed, especially everything that is beautiful, everything that is noble, and the love of those who love me. I will also do my best to use each gift of life to some good purpose, first by loving, especially those who are near but also, in so far as I can, all of those whom God loves. Then I will try to do as much good as I can, like writing these reflections. For me, that is what it means to choose life.

I know perfectly well that a day will come when the gift of life will not be there for me. I believe that there will be another gift there for me instead. I hope to be able to receive that gift, as I have received the gift of life, with joyful anticipation. But until that day, I will choose life.

Prayer: Yes. I choose life.

Job 43

In the days when the Bible was being written, much of Jewish piety was dominated by the belief that, if you do what is right, God will prosper you. This belief is dominant in the book of Proverbs and in other places as well. There is truth in that belief. But it has its limitations. The book of Job was included in the Bible to help people recognize the limitations of their popular belief.

The book tells a story. It is a drama. The protagonist in the story is Job, a very righteous and wealthy man. He had houses and cattle and many children whom he loved dearly. In the drama, Satan challenges God by saying that Job is only righteous because he is wealthy. God allows Satan to test Job by taking away everything that he had, even his children. Job is plunged into spiritual turmoil. Job's friends come, supposedly to comfort him. But they really only torment him with the traditional wisdom that says, since God prospers the righteous, Job must have done something wrong. Job insists that he has done nothing to deserve his misfortune and calls on God to come and reckon with him. The dramatic interaction stretches over thirty seven chapters of the Bible. Finally, God does come and speaks to Job through a whirl wind. Though God does not answer Job's questions directly, he helps Job to catch a new understanding of the shape of reality. Job repents of his protests and stands humbly before God. Then God restores Job's fortune, giving him even more wealth and more children than he had before.

The book speaks so deeply of the human condition that it has been rewritten in modern form by such authors as Archibald McLiesch and Paul Simon. I once tried my own hand at writing a chancel drama meant to reflect on the meaning of the book. I want to share a portion of it with you in the form of a short story. The scene is set on the balcony of Job's house two years after God restored Job's lost fortune. (It will help if you have read the book of Job.)

Job's wife finds Job standing on the balcony of his house at the end of a work day. He is gazing at the cultivated fields. She says, "Well here you are in your favorite place again. Are you ready for some iced tea and company?"

Job answers, "Yes definitely. Both. It sure is good to see the land being productive again. I am glad we did not lose the land while we were losing everything else. Look, the wheat will soon be ready to harvest. Isn't it beautiful?"

"You seem to be feeling good."

"Grateful. That is what I am. At least I have learned to be grateful."

"Everybody around here admires your success. They call you the comeback kid."

"I know. But they don't have the foggiest notion what life is all about."

"They wanted you to tell them when they asked you to speak at the civic club."

"Yes, but they didn't like what I told them: 'hard work, good agricultural practices, sound management and still be ready to lose it all in case something beyond your control goes haywire.' They didn't want to hear that. They wanted some kind of a magical secret of success, some way of guaranteeing that nothing will ever go wrong."

"I think they wanted you to give them some religious secret to success."

"Humph! Their problem is that they don't know the difference between religion and superstition."

"But Job, you are a religious man."

"Oh you bet I am. After that conversation with the whirlwind, I will always be religious. I will never forget for a moment that God is God and God is always at work around me in ways that I will never be able to even begin to understand. But I would never try to manage God. I would never try to put a bit and bridle on God. "

"Your friends made it pretty rough on you during the bad times."

"Yeah, but they meant well. They were just trying to stick up for God—as if God needed anyone to stick up for him."

"I made things rough for you too, telling you to curse God and die."

I just knew you were feeling the same things I was feeling. You didn't know it but you were the only one who was really still with me."

"We really have been through a lot, haven't we Job."

"Yes we have. Say, how are the children."

"They are coming along fine. They are even learning to call us Mom and Dad. It was a great idea just adopt all of the orphans in the county."

"When you lose everything, you learn to feel for those who never had anything. I feel like they are our real family. I believe they will grow up to be really fine people. "

"Job, please don't misunderstand. I love our new family. But some times I miss our own children so much that I can hardly stand it."

"I understand. I feel the same way. Just yesterday, I was thinking about the time when Rachel was little and she—she—Rachel."

Suddenly Job is overcome with grief. He sits down, buries his face in his hands, and begins to sob. His wife comes and puts her arms around him and cries with him. The figures on the stage go still and a tall figure robed and hooded in burlap comes and stands between us and the couple on the stage and speaks.

"Yes Job. You understand. You are beginning to see everything as I see it. I don't know why I thought that would be such a great thing for you but I did. Life is not all planned out. It develops as it happens. It is full of possibilities, good ones and others. I can make some things happen—and so can you—but we have to work with the happenings. I had to make the world that way because it is the only kind of world in which you can live a life like mine. It is the only kind of world in which your actions can have real significance. There has to be the possibility of badness so there can be the possibility of real goodness. There has to be the possibility of hate so there can be the possibility of real love. There has to be a possibility of war so there can be a possibility of real peace. In a world like that, you can live a life that is really significant, a life that can make a difference. You did not curse me while you were going through your bad times. But if you had, I wouldn't have killed you like you thought I would. I put you through that. And I went through it with you. When you go through something like that, I go through it with you. Right now, I am going through grief with you. I have been through lots of things with lots of people. I understand.

When anything can happen, sometimes bad things happen. And that guy Satan, he is just a function of the system. Some times the bad things come at us in force and try to break us. Yes, I said us. Can you believe that happens to me too? It happens to me when it happens to you.

But believe it or not Job, you are getting the benefit of things being like they are. You are learning to love. Real love only grows in the push and pull of life. And love is the real prize in life. That is the way in which I want you to be like me. I want you to love like I love.

I put things together as they are because I love you. I know that is hard for you to understand. Some day, at the right time, I am going to have to come over there where you are and live a life like yours to show you how to live in love under your circumstances—and to show you how much I love you—and to help you see that life and all that goes with it is a gift given in love."

At just this time, Satan enters, walking boldly, obviously in a jovial mood. He says" Well, Lord, I have to hand it to you. You won that bet. You were right about Job. He never did curse you. But he was one in a million. Anyone else would have…"

At this time, God turns to face Satan and us and we are able to see that his face is blackened with ashes and that there are streaks where tears have washed the ashes away. Satan is shocked. He says, ":What is this? Almighty God in sack cloth and ashes? Almighty God in grief?"

God retorts, "Get out of my sight you son of a …"

Prayer: Lord: help me to understand.

Don't Sweat the Small Stuff

"Vanity of Vanities, all is vanity" and "chasing after the wind". These are the words of Qoheleth, the teacher—or preacher, who wrote the book of Ecclesiastes. Ecclesiastes is one of the books of wisdom in the Old Testament. These words are a refrain that runs through most of the book. As a result, many people think of Ecclesiastes as the most cynical book in the Hebrew Scriptures. But I think that is a misunderstanding of the message.

Qoheleth speaks of the things that most people value most highly and strive to achieve, the things in which many people invest their energies and their lives. He speaks of wealth and power and pleasure and wisdom. He says that trying to achieve those things is like trying to catch the wind. He even assumes the character of Solomon, who, in the minds of the first readers of this book, had achieved more wealth and more power and more pleasure and more wisdom than anyone else they knew. Qoheleth has Solomon to tell us that these things are all vanity.

I think I understand what Qoheleth is trying to tell us. He is an old man. He has done a lot of living. He wants to tell us what he has learned. Well, I suppose that, all things being considered, I am an old man too. I think I understand what he is trying to say. I have never achieved wealth or power. But I have set some goals that were ambitious for me and worked hard to try to achieve them. I have achieved some successes. But the successes have never been as exciting or as satisfying as I had hoped they would be. In fact, most of my successes have left me feeling more tired than triumphant. As a student of philosophy and theology, I have intentionally sought wisdom. I think that is something we should all do. But in all of my seeking after wisdom, I have discovered it is true that, the wider the circle of your knowledge grows, the wider the perimeter on which you confront the unknown. And, the more you understand, the more you know how limited your understanding is. Yes, we should all seek wisdom, but we may as well know from the outset that it will be like trying to catch the wind.

I think Qoheleth is trying to tell us, "Don't sweat the small stuff." Then I think he is trying to tell us that most of the stuff that most people think is big stuff is really small stuff. So what if you retire as CEO of your company. The sun will still rise and set as it always has and the rivers will run pretty much where they have always run. Put things into perspective. Don't give things more attention than they deserve. Don't hang your hopes on things that are likely to disappoint you. There is real liberation in being able follow that advice.

But, I think that is only half of the message of Qoheleth. Qohwleth wants to tell us that the things most people think are big stuff are really small stuff. But he eventually gets around to telling us that the things most people think are small stuff are really big stuff. The everyday experiences that most people take for granted are the very things that can be most satisfying for us if we learn to receive them gratefully and enjoy them fully. He lists: daily food and drink, daily work, friendship, the companionship of a spouse, and a relationship with God.

Here is what I think Qoheleth really wants to tell us: "Go eat your bread with enjoyment and drink your wine with a merry heart; for God has long ago approved what you do. Let your garments always be white and do not let oil be lacking on your head. Enjoy life with the wife whom you love, all the days of your vain life that are given to you under the sun, for that is your portion in life and in the toil with which you toil under the sun. Whatever your hand finds to do, do it with all your might…(Ecclesiastes 9:7-10a)

I believe that the book of Ecclesiastes brings us one of the best pieces of good news in the Old Testament. It is simply this; real satisfaction is to be found, not in those elusive prizes that most people strive for but very few people can achieve. Real satisfaction, real blessedness, comes from making the most of those every day gifts that God puts into most of our hands. With what is left of my life, I will choose significant goals and work at them, not for what they will gain for me, but simply because they are worth doing. I will look for my happiness in enjoying every day of my life as a good gift from God.

Prayer: Thank you, Lord, for daily work—and bread—and love.

Promises, Promises

When we think about what it means to do what is right, many of us think first of the Ten Commandments. (We do that in spite of the fact that most of us can't remember what the Ten Commandments are.) The Ten Commandments are important. But in the context of the biblical faith, they play a role that is different—and much bigger—than the role most of us assign to them.

Just so you can remember what we are talking about, here are the Ten Commandments in an abbreviated form. (You can read them in their fuller form, and in their context, from Exodus 20:1-17 and Deuteronomy 5:1-21). Here they are: You shall have no other gods before the one true God. You shall not worship idols. You shall not make wrongful use of the Lord's name. You shall keep the Sabbath day holy. You shall honor your father and mother. You shall not kill. You shall not commit adultery. You shall not steal. You shall not bear false witness against your neighbor. You shall not covet.

Many people think of these commandments as prerequisites, things you have to do to win God's approval and love. But, in fact, they were given to the people of Israel after God had already chosen them and saved them from slavery in Egypt. They were a gift from God that was a sign of the covenant, not a prerequisite. High expectations are a compliment, an expression of love.

But, when we put the commandments into the context of the New Testament faith, they take on additional functions. It is God's way with us that God required of us what is really good for us and then enables us to do what is required. The commandments take on three functions. First, they do indeed tell us what we ought to do. They describe the truly good life that we ought to live. But when we take them seriously as Jesus taught us to take them, as having to do with our inner lives as well as our outward motions, (Matthew 5:17-48) then the Ten Commandments show us that we fall far short of being what we ought to be. They can and should make us want to be better people than we are. Then, finally, the Ten Commandments show us the life that we can live if we let God's saving love work in our lives. Yes, if we will live our lives in an open and responsive relationship with God, God will make a big difference in our lives. The Ten Commandments become ten promises.

Did you ever think of the Ten Commandments as ten promises? Look at them again. You can read them that way. And they can be very precious promises indeed.

For a person who is plagued by stress and frustration that cause violent impulses to rise up within him, "You shall not kill" can be a precious promise.

For a person who values his or her marriage but is often exposed to temptation to do things our culture has come to condone, it can be very encouraging to hear the promise, "You shall not commit adultery."

And how great it could be to claim the promise, "You shall not covet." Our culture has made coveting a way of life. Our culture cultivates a jealousy and unhappiness that keeps us wanting more. It makes us unhappy when we have every reason to be happy. And it can make a real mess out of our economy—witness the current crisis in home mortgages. How precious is the promise that we can be happy with what we have.

But Jesus said there are two commandments that sum up all of the others. Remember? "You shall love the Lord your God with all your heart, and with all your soul, and with all your mind, and with all your strength." And "You shall love your neighbor as you love yourself (Mark 12:28-31). These are the most precious promises of all. The next several meditations will be about the way in which those promises can be fulfilled.

Prayer: Now, this is something new to me, Lord. Help me to see where it will lead me.

Learning to Love

Reflections on the Prelude to the Bible, Genesis 1-3

It's About Love

"What the world needs now is love sweet love. That's the only thing there's just too little of." So said a once popular song. And something deep inside of many of us responded. "Yes!" Love is really what life is about. It seems to take some of us a long time to figure that out. Eventually, the realization dawns that, unless there is love in our lives, we are not really alive. And unless there is love in the world—or because there is not enough love in the world—the world is in deep trouble. Life is about love.

The Christian faith is about love too. No, it is not about being good or being right or going to heaven when you die. It is not about church growth or the politics of the right or of the left. These things are important but they are not what it is about. Jesus has told us what it is really all about. He said that the two commandments that sum up all of the others are these. "You shall love the Lord your God with all your heart and with all your soul and with all your mind and with all your strength. And you shall love your neighbor as you love yourself." (Mark 12:28-31) He even went further in the Sermon on the Mount. He said, "Be perfect, therefore, as your heavenly Father is perfect." (Matthew 5:48) In the context of this passage, that means that we are to learn to love like God loves. What a role model! Wow!

It's about love. But we have some problems with that. First, many of us really don't know what love is. If we count on the television soap operas to show us what love is, we will be in serious trouble. They seem to tell us that love is a selfish thing that is full of hurtfulness and jealousy. At its best, our culture usually represents love to be either sexual attraction or a warm fuzzy feeling. There has got to be more to it than that. Our second problem is that, if we catch a bigger vision of what love is, many of us may not really want to live in love. Our culture has given us some agendas that do not leave much room for love. And finally, if we decide that we really do want to love, many of us may find that we just don't have love within ourselves to give.

If we get serious about loving, we will find that the Bible can be a tremendous resource for us. The Bible is a love story. From the beginning to the end, it is the story of how God's love works itself out in life and history. Yes, there are large parts of the Bible that seem to be about anything but love. They are full of conflict and violence. But life is often full of conflict and violence. When love has to work in situations like that—and it often does—it can't always come out looking pretty. Taken as a whole, the Bible tells us how God loves. That can teach us how we ought to love. We are going to explore that. There will be some surprises. The Bible can also put us in touch with God's love for us so that God can love us into both the desire and the ability to love.

If we want to find our way into love, it will be best for us to start by trying to learn how to give love. That is not where most of us want to start. We are more interested in learning how to get love. A number of years ago, a psychologist named Harville Hendrix wrote a book entitled *Getting the Love You Want*, (New York, Harper and Rowe, 1990). The title did not really represent the contents of the book but it made the book a best seller. It got the author interviewed on Opra Winfrey's television show twice. Lots of us are eager to get love. And, when love is flourishing, it involves both receiving and giving love. Both are important. The two feed on each other. But if we start by trying to get love for ourselves, that effort is likely to lead us down all kinds of wrong paths. It will be better for us to start by trying to learn to give love.

It will help if we can start by getting a basic understanding of what love is. If we are to take God as our role model, we can look at a very familiar verse of scripture and ask what love is in that context. "God so loved the world that he gave his only Son, so that everyone who believes in him may not perish but have eternal life." (John 3:16) What is love in that context? Isn't it a commitment? We don't want to hear that. We don't like to make commitments. Lots of people today are trying to invent a kind of love that does not involve commitment. But it doesn't work. Love is commitment. It is wanting for the one who is loved, or the ones who are loved, what is really best. It is being willing to do for those who are loved whatever is necessary to make it possible for the loved ones to have the life that really is life. That kind of commitment can be costly. God's commitment was—and is.

But the commitment needs to be made joyfully, not grudgingly. It should be like the love that parents have for their children, a love that values those who are loved and finds delight in them.

How is this for a definition of love? "Love is a joyful commitment of life to life." Now we are going to work our way through parts of the Bible to see how love takes shape in all of the different situations of life and how it can happen in our lives.

Prayer: I have finally figured out what I should pray for. Lord, teach me to love.

Where Love Begins

Now, we are going to try to learn to love. If we take the advice of Jesus, we will let God be our role model. (Matthew 5:43-48) We are going to try to learn to love as God loves. We are going to start with the first chapter in the great story of God's love, the first chapter of the book of Genesis, the first book in the Bible. It will be helpful to recognize at the outset that the things this story tells us about are not happenings that could have been recorded with a camcorder if a photographer had been hiding behind the right bush at the right time. It is not that kind of story. But it is the story that Spirit led people of faith chose as the prelude to the whole collection of Hebrew Scriptures. It is a story that is full of meaning that has interpreted life for people of many cultures for several thousand years. We will go to that story and ask what it can tell us about how God loves and how we should love.

In the beginning, whom did God love? In the beginning, since there was no one but God, God must have loved God. Now there is a surprise. After years of being told that we should not love ourselves, it is a little surprising to learn that God's love must have begun with self love. But it is not surprising to the social scientists. They have known for a long time that people who are not able to love themselves with a healthy self love probably will not be able to love anyone else.

Our problem is that we have too often confused self love with selfishness. Those two are not the same. In fact, they are opposites. Selfishness is an anxious, greedy little attitude that centers everything in self and draws everything toward that center. It makes the selfish person shrink up into something smaller and smaller. Self love, on the other hand, is a joyful affirmation of self that sets us free from anxiety and fills us with love for life. It makes us bigger persons and overflows in a vitality that reaches out beyond self.

Can we imagine God modeling a joyful commitment of life to God's own life? Can we imagine God wanting what is good for God's self and giving God's self to making what is good to happen? Yes, I think that is a proper way of reading the story that Genesis 1 tells. We will soon see that God's love overflows in creative action that causes other realities to come into being. We will eventually learn that God's love can be self giving, even sacrificial. But no one can really give self unless that one has first claimed self. God could not reach out in love for others unless God had first loved self—and neither can we.

But is that something we can really do? Are we able to love ourselves? Some of us may not be able to love ourselves. Most of us who can love ourselves were loved into the ability to do that by growing up in loving homes. But some people were not that fortunate. Some grew up in environments in which relationships were unhealthy—or abusive—or exploitative. Some grew up among people who wanted to love but were not able. And some who were blessed with loving relationships in their childhood have been subjected to harsh experiences in life that have beaten all of the self respect out of them. And some of us have done things that have left us unable to love ourselves. If we are not able to love ourselves, we desperately need to get in touch with some love that will love us into the ability to love ourselves.

Where can we find such an enabling love? The Bible tells us that God loves us. One of the recurrent themes in the book of Psalms says, "O give thanks to the Lord for he is good. His steadfast love endures for ever." (Psalm 107 and others) The New Testament tells us that God has shown us God's love for us in Jesus Christ. (1 John 4:7-12 and others) But that information is really not enough. We need to find some experiences in life through which God's love can come through to us, in human relationships. Some people try to meet that need by going on a romantic quest for a dream lover whom they hope will make everything beautiful in their lives. That is almost certain to lead to disappointment in one way or another. It will be wiser to intentionally get in touch with as many expressions of God's love as you can, in family relationships, in real friendships, in caring fellowships, in the appreciation of the daily gift of life.

During the nineteen seventies, when the nation wide recession finally came to Houston, the center of the country's petro-chemical industry, something happened that represented sacrificial love to all who heard of it. Many companies that served the industry had to "downsize" in order to survive. Many very capable people were forced into unemployment. This was an especially harsh experience for the engineers. These highly trained and very sophisticated people were accustomed to being sought after by the industry. But, during the recession, many found themselves being unemployed through no fault of their own. And it was very difficult for them to find employment. There were few engineering jobs and other companies were reluctant to hire people who were well along in their careers or who were "overqualified."

In that situation, one company that hired a large staff of engineers chose one of their most able young engineers and put him in charge of "outplacement". As it became necessary for the company to reduce staff, it would be his job to decide which engineers to let go and, if possible, to help them find employment with other companies. Can you imagine a more painful thing to have to do? It became more and more painful as the recession continued. Finally, the young engineer found that there were only two engineers left, and one of them had to go. He knew that the job was his for the taking and that, if he took it, he would be assured of employment as long as the company survived. But the other engineer was an older man who had actually been his mentor early in his career. He was only a few years from retirement and would certainly be considered overqualified. Finding a job would be practically impossible for him—and he had two children in college. The engineer in charge of outplacement thought about the decision he had to make for a long time. Then the engineer in charge of outplacement outplaced himself. The story of what he had done circulated rapidly in the community of technical people. It represented something beautifully human in a harsh situation. It gave many people the inspiration they needed to keep on trusting and hoping.

Wherever real love is, there is God's love coming through. One of the most important things we can do is to find ways of getting in touch with God's love for us, to receive it gratefully and joyfully, to take it into ourselves, and to let it work in our lives to make us able to love ourselves. That is important because that is where love begins.

Prayer: Lord, help me to experience your love.

Love Creates

If we take God as our role model for loving, we will find an exciting picture of what love is in the first chapter of the biblical book of Genesis. There, we see God being committed to God's own life in a love that builds through dynamic interactions until it overflows and reaches out. It has to have some others to love. Since there were no others, God called into being some others whom God could love—a whole universe of others.

God wants to love us into that same kind of love that overflows in creative love for others. Again, the pictures of the universe sent back to us by the Hovel telescope come to mind, a universe that is vast beyond our ability to imagine. When we think of all that God has created and is creating, we are likely to say, "Hey, there is no way that I can do that." No, we can't. We do have some mechanical and artistic abilities that allow us to participate in small ways in God's ongoing work of creating the physical world. But that is not really the most magnificent part of God's creative work. The most magnificent part of the work of God's creative love is the work that God does to bring human personhood and community into being. And that is something in which we can participate.

God chose to call us into being as persons who are, in certain important ways, created in the image of God. That calls for a certain kind of creative work. It cannot be accomplished simply by action. It has to be accomplished by interaction. A very wise man, (Emerito Nacphil) once observed that the creation story does not picture God ordering things into existence. It pictures God inviting things into existence. God makes a space for the thing to be created, God creates the possibility. Then God says, "Let there be… " In this way, God allows the things coming into existence to participate in their own creation.

That must certainly be true of human personhood and human community. Two human beings may have the biological ability to produce a baby. But that is just the beginning. The much bigger task is to surround that baby with the relationships of a human family and of a human community that will enable the baby to grow into a whole, mature person. That will require a lifetime of loving interaction.

Certainly you know how that works. Haven't you ever experienced some relationships that seem to invite your personhood into existence and some others that seem determined to snuff it out? The Jewish philosopher, Martin Buber, described two different kinds of relationships. He said there are "I-it" relationships in which we treat some other as an inanimate object. Then there are "I-thou" relationships in which we treat another as a person like ourselves. Buber says that "I-thou" relationships evoke personhood in both the person who is being related to and in the person who is doing the relating. (*I and Thou*, New York, Charles Scribner's Sons, 1970)

Let me tell you a true story. Two sisters went back to visit the city where they had both grown up after one of them had been away for forty years. Many things had changed, but some had not. The old house, in which they had lived when they were growing up, was still there. Memories came flooding back in torrents. Behind the house, they could still see the mom and pop service station that had been there when they were young. That brought to mind the memory of the saddest day in their lives, the day when their mother died. They had both been very young. They remembered how the mother of the family that ran the service station had come and taken them home to care for them through their grief.

The sisters drove around to the front of the service station. To their surprise, the same family name was still on the sign. They stopped and asked the attendant if the same family was still running the service station and, if they were, if the woman who had been so kind to them was still living. The attendant said that he was the son of that family and that his mother was sitting just inside the station. The sisters went in. They found a very feeble old lady sitting in a chair in the corner of the station. She was blind. She must have felt totally useless. The sisters introduced themselves. The old lady remembered. Then the sisters told her how very important her loving care had been to them. They told her that they had never forgotten her kindness. As they spoke, tears ran down from sightless eyes and an old lady who was feeling like a nobody had her personhood evoked and validated. She knew that she was someone. She experienced creation.

When relationships and communities come into being and evoke and express personhood, creation happens. The mark of true personhood is the ability to love. We can participate with God in that work of creation.

That is a part of God's creative plan. I have heard people saying that they were afraid that they might sin by loving their children or some other person more than they love God. That is not something we have to worry about. There is a place in the Bible that says God is a jealous God, (Exodus 20:5) but that means we must not love anything else instead of God. When we love those whom God loves, we are expressing our love for God. Real love in inclusive, not competitive. Love should become for us a whole way of relating to life. God wants the circle of our love to grow wider so that we can participate with God in the work of creation.

Prayer: Lord, help me to recognize the opportunities you give me to participate in your creative love.

Love Provides

The first chapter of the Bible makes us stretch our imagination to catch a vision of the awesome reality of God setting us an example of love, an example that teaches us to love ourselves with an expansive love that will overflow in creative outreach to others. By contrast, the next two chapters of the Bible tell a very down to earth story. It is the story of God's love for Adam and Eve. Again, these are not stories of happenings that could ever have been recorded on a camcorder. But they are stories that can tell us a lot about what it means to love.

The first thing we can learn from this story is that love provides. Right after telling us again that God created man, the Bible tells us that "…the Lord God planted a garden in Eden in the east and there he put the man whom he had formed. Out of the ground the Lord God made to grow every tree that is pleasing to the sight and good for food… " (Genesis 2:8-9) So God gave man food to eat and the other physical things needed to sustain life. God also gave beauty to enrich life. But that is not all. God gave man a responsible role to play in the scheme of things. "The Lord God took the man and put him in the Garden of Eden to till it and keep it." (Genesis 2:15) Man was created to be a partner with God in the care of creation. A little later, we read that God gave the man a human companion, a gift of relatedness and of community. (Genesis 2:18-25) There is one other thing that God gave to the man and to the woman. God gave them a relationship with God. As the story develops, we will see that this relationship was not just a passive relationship. It was an ongoing active interaction. God gave to the man and to the woman everything they would need to live the fully human life for which God created them.

Now, you have already guessed that I am going to tell you that you should provide for those whom you love the things they will need. But there is something you need to know before you get to that. God has provided for you the things you need for fullness of life. In this story, Adam and Eve represent both you and those others to whom you should relate in love. It is important to realize that God is providing for you food, beauty, responsibility, relatedness and all of the other things you need to live a fully human life—including an ongoing relationship with the living God. Whether we realize it or not, God is always reaching out to relate to us in active love. We are very foolish when we boast that "We have earned everything we have ever gotten and no one has ever given us anything." We impoverish and disable ourselves when we make that boast. It is important for us to learn to relate ourselves to life and to the God who meets us in life in gratitude. Gratitude both frees us and enables us to express our love by providing for those whom we love. Gratitude is a profound kind of happiness that is always available to us.

Having said that, we are ready to say that we should do what we can to provide for those whom we love the things that they need. Every parent knows that comes naturally. But there are some things we need to learn about providing.

The first thing we need to learn is that love provides those things that are needed for fullness of life. Too many of us get caught up in giving those whom we love the things that have to do with what our culture calls "the good life"—that is, the life of material prosperity, rather than the things needed for what God calls the good life, that is the life of love. The tragedy of our age is that so many parents so exhaust themselves in trying to give their children "the better things" that they do not have enough of themselves left to give their children the best thing, a loving relationship with their parents.

I know of a family that is an inspiration to me because, all things being considered, I think they have got it right. This is a "blended family." When they came together they were seven people, each with injuries that had to be overcome. The husband and wife worked hard to provide for the children. But they gave priority to the human aspects of their life together. Each of the children was a unique individual with unique gifts and needs. Parenting was a challenge. The parents had to accept the children where they were, to stand by their sides, even when they got into trouble, to set expectations when they were needed and to give support in appropriate ways. Parenting was hard work. It led the parents through many bewildering and difficult situations. Lots of accepting and forgiving has been necessary. Now the children are grown. It would be hard to imagine a group with more unique personalities. But they love each other. When they are together, it is easy to see that their gathering is a place where love is.

As our circle of love enlarges and includes all of those whom God loves, providing becomes more complex. The circle will eventually include many poor and oppressed people. What should we do when famine overtakes the people of some country on the other side of the world and we see the faces of starving children gazing at us from the covers of news magazines. Obviously we cannot provide personally all of the things they need. But we must never forget their needs and we should commit ourselves to reorganizing things in the world so that everyone can have enough. It is entirely possible for us to wipe out world hunger in our life time. Yes, it really is. Loving people will look for ways to participate in doing that.

But, providing for the physical needs of the poor can not be the whole story. The lives we see being lived by the affluent people of the world does not suggest that material prosperity itself would lead people to fullness of life. Providing will always be a more complex process—and it will always require some response, some interaction—and that can be very demanding.

To love is to want what is best for those who are loved and to be willing to do what can be done to make that possible. To love as God loves is to want what is best for all people and to be willing to do what can be done to make that possible.

Prayer: Lord, help me to know what I should try to give to those whom I love.

Love Has High Expectations

Shel Silverstine wrote a children's book, probably for adults, that is called "The Giving Tree." (New York, Harper and Row, 1964) It tells a story about a boy's relationship with a certain apple tree. The tree always gave the boy all that he wanted. The boy played in its branches and ate its fruit. As a youth, the boy sat in the tree's shade. The tree kept giving and the boy kept taking. At no time did the boy accept any responsibility for caring for the tree or giving anything back to it. Finally, as an adult, the boy cut the tree down and used it for lumber to build himself a house. The story ends with the boy as a tired old man, needing a place to rest. He sits down on the stump that is all that is left of the tree. Some people say that the total sacrifice of the tree is an example of true love.

I think there is something wrong with that picture. There is something wrong with any relationship that leaves one party spoiled and the other spent. That is really not the shape of the love of which God has set us an example. Yes, the love of God is sacrificial—and our love may have to be sacrificial too. But there are also expectations in the love of God. In Genesis 2:15-17, we are reminded that God put the man in the garden to till it and keep it, to be God's partner in the care of the creation. The man had certain responsibilities. Then, there are certain responsibilities related to man's relationship with God represented by God's order that the man and the woman must not eat the fruit of one certain tree. As the story develops, God eventually enters into a two way covenant relationship with all people in which there are to be both gifts and expectations on both sides. God knows that the expectations are important. It is important for us to know that the God who comes to meet us in life has certain expectations that we will have to live up to. Only so can we grow into the kind of people God wants us to be, people who are able to love.

Then what should we expect of those whom we love: our parents, our children, our marriage partners, our friends, the strangers to whom we are told we should reach out in love, yes, and even the enemies whom God calls us to love? We should expect those whom we love to live up to their own highest potential as human beings. We should expect them to be responsible participants in the ongoingness of life in the world. That is just a part of wanting for those whom we love what is best for them.

We should also expect those whom we love to respect our personhood as we respect theirs. To be realistic, every really important relationship is going to require some forgiving and some allowing for the other's need to grow in their ability to love. But ultimately, there must be a mutuality of respect. If we allow ourselves to be drawn into sick relationships with others or with life in which we give up our healthy love for ourselves, then the liberating and enabling forces within us that enable us to reach out to others in love will eventually wither away.

Let this be said very plainly. There is nothing in the Bible that says anyone must willingly stay in an abusive relationship that threatens his or her life or personhood.

High expectations are a precious gift when given in love. No, we should not heap unrealistic expectations upon those whom we love—or on ourselves. And when we have high expectations of those whom we love, we should be ready to do what we can to help them live up to those expectations. That is the shape of God's relationship with us. But with those provisions, high expectations are a gift of love. They help us to become all that we can be.

It is true that, if we have high expectations of another, we make ourselves vulnerable to disappointment. We will soon learn that vulnerability is an aspect of love. We will have to learn to forgive and to accept and to seek healing for ourselves.

Prayer: Thank you, Lord, for expecting much of us, and teach us what we should expect of others.

Love Lets Go

God created us to live in a very special relationship with God's self—which is also a very special relationship with life as a whole—a relationship in which God provides and we trust, a relationship in which God has high expectations and we try to live up to them, a relationship in which God loves us and we respond by loving God and all that God loves. But God wants us to live in that life shaping relationship because we have chosen to. It just wouldn't be real any other way. For that reason, God has put our lives into our hands and trusted us with the freedom and the responsibility to decide what we will do with them.

In Genesis 3:1-7, there is a story about Adam and Eve being tempted by the serpent to choose another way of life, a way different from the life for which they were created. There are always those temptations. You know that, don't you? And God allowed Adam and Eve carry on their conversation with the tempter and to make their decision as if God were not present. Of course, God is always present. God knows what we are thinking and doing. But God gives us the freedom to decide as if God were not present.

Eric From, the psychologist whose book, *The Art of Loving* has become a classic, emphasizes that love is a very close relationship in which two people can become one and yet remain separate so that each person has integrity. (New York, Harper and Row, 1956) God wants that kind of relationship with us because God wants to call us into being as unique persons. And we should want that kind of relationship with the people whom we love.

The theologian, Miroslav Volf, says that says that love can be represented by a drama with four acts that can be represented by four postures. The first posture is one of opening your arms to invite another into your embrace. The second is one of standing and waiting for the other to come into your embrace. The third is one of closing your arms to embrace one who has chosen to embrace you. The fourth is opening your arms again so that the other is free to move and live his or her own life. (*Exclusion & Embrace,* Nashville, Abingdon, 1996)

I saw this kind of love dramatized in one particular family that had love to share. The father was an industrial worker. The mother was a part time teacher's aid. The two children were high school students. Because they realized that they had love to share, they volunteered to be foster parents. They took three young children from a dysfunctional family into their home. They treated them like parts of their own family. They loved them. They worked with them to help them overcome the results of their first family's deficiencies. They took them with them wherever they went. They dressed them up and took them to church and on family outings. They helped them discover what a healthy family can be like. They did everything that a loving family would do for young children. The children thrived. They were with their new family for more than a year and they grew very close. But when the time came for it they did the most difficult thing of all. When adoptive parents were found for the children, the foster family let them go.

Such respect for the autonomy of the other can be risky, especially when we are talking about our relationships with our children or with others who have been very important to us. They may choose to live a life that is different from the truly good life we want for them. They may choose something other than a loving relationship with us. That is what Adam and Eve did. Of course, God's relationship with others is different from ours in one very important way. God knows what is best for us and for others. We may not. We must always be open to the possibility that the other will know better than we what is really best for them. That complicates things—but it is part of a healthy loving relationship.

But what if the one whom we love chooses a way that really is the wrong way, a way that is destructive to him or her and to others—or to you? Then things get really complicated. We will think about that next.

Prayer: Help me to love and let go.

Love Follows

Once I became acquainted with a group of people who were parents of drug abusing teenagers. They had tried everything they knew to bring their children back to a healthy life style. They were always there to bail their children out of jail and to "pad the sharp corners" to keep their children from getting hurt. But nothing worked. The parents lived in constant turmoil because of the disruption of their own lives and in constant anxiety about their children. Nothing was working. Eventually these parents came to realize that their well intentioned efforts were actually enabling their children to continue in a self-destructive life style. In desperation, they adopted an approach called "Tough Love". They told their children that they loved them and that they would do anything for them except to enable them to go on living in a self-destructive way. They told their children that they could continue to live in the family home and to be supported by their parents only if they gave up their drug abuse. If they continued to use drugs, they would have to get out of the home and try to make life work on their own. Their ultimatum was, "straight or the streets." The parents hoped that, by forcing their children to reckon with the results of their own decisions and actions, the children would make discoveries that would cause them to choose a healthy life style.

When I first heard that story, I was horrified. I could not imagine how any loving parent could do that to his or her own children. Then I remembered the story that the Bible tells in Genesis 3. In the story, Adam and Eve, who represent both us and those whom we are called to love, had chosen a way of life that is different from the truly good life for which God had created them, (us). God allowed them to follow the way they had chosen, but they had to get out of the Garden of Eden, the place of God's perfect providence. They would have to reckon with the results of their own decisions and actions.

There are two lessons that we can learn from this story. We can learn to look honestly at the things that are going wrong in our lives and in our world and ask if they are at least in part the results of our decisions and actions. We can ask if those discoveries call for changes in our lives. That is really hard to do. The other lesson is even harder. It is that we sometimes have to let those whom we love follow their own ways even if we know they are making mistakes so that they can discover their wrongness by experiencing the results of their own decisions and actions. That is really difficult, especially when we are dealing with those who are closest to us.

But, is that the end of the story of God's love and of ours? Is it just "My way or the highway"? No, if we follow the story, we will find that God kept on loving his wayward creatures. Genesis 3:21 tells us that God actually made garments for the man and the woman before they were exiled from Eden. God required them to go, but God packed them a suit case for the journey. And God kept following, always at a distance that kept God from taking away their autonomy, always looking for ways in which God could work through the experiences and interactions of their lives to win them back to the life for which they were created.

There are all kinds of difficulties in this kind of loving. One of the biggest is the danger that the people we love will interpret acceptance as approval. In order to keep a loving relationship open, we may have to forgive the wrongness we see in others and decide not to let that terminate a loving relationship. We will have to accept the fact that things are as they are and accept other people as they are. But it is also important for us to keep communicating our high expectations. Otherwise the others may interpret our acceptance as permission or even approval. We will need to be intentional about communicating both the acceptance and the expectations. Sometimes the others will not want it that way. They may turn and walk away from a relationship that they interpret as disapproval. Then we must find ways to keep on following, to keep on keeping the possibility of a redemptive relationship open.

The parts of the Bible that follow the first chapters tell how God kept on reaching out to his people through the happenings of their lives and of history to win them back to the way of love. The stories of wars, oppression, political subterfuge and corruption and of personal waywardness and suffering do not sound much like stories of love—but they are. They are stories of how God reaches out to his people and tries to save them, (and us), under all kinds of different circumstances. Even the Bible writers probably sometimes misunderstood what God was trying to do. But when the later rabbis assembled the literature of the Hebrew Scriptures, they chose the stories in the first chapters of Genesis to help us understand what was really happening in the rest of the Bible.

What would it mean for us to keep on following and reaching out in love to those who have chosen ways that are destructive to themselves and others—and maybe even to us? What would it mean for us to keep on reaching out to a world that has chosen the wrong way? There is no simple answer to that question. But it is a question that must be the constant companion of one who has chosen to live in love.

Now we are ready to move on to learn from another story. That story tells us more about how God continues to reach out to us and to those whom we love. It is a story that brings us hope for ourselves and shows us even more about how to do the hard work of loving. That story revolves around the life of a man named Jesus.

Prayer: Lord, help me to see you following me and to turn and follow you.

Meeting the Savior

Reflections on the witnesses of the New

Testament writers about the ways in

which God reaches out to us to save.

Jesus

At a crucial time in the history of the people of Israel, and at a crucial time in the history of the world, God reached out to perform a great pivotal work for the salvation of humankind. He did that work through a young teacher named Jesus from the Jewish town of Nazareth. Jesus was a real person. He was human just as we are. His life was, in many ways, like ours. And yet God worked in a very special way in and through that person and the event that was his life. Through him, God made possible fullness of life for all people and also the new age of peace on earth that we all yearn for. Since that time, the faithful have been saying and singing, "Jesus saves."

But we may want to ask, how can that be? How can someone who lived two thousand years ago make a difference in my life today? How can someone who lived in an ancient society on the other side of the world make a difference when my marriage is in trouble, or when I can't find a job so I can support my family? How can someone who lived so long ago make a difference in the political tensions that are developing today in the very place where he lived and threatening the world with destructive war? These are good questions and it is important for us to find an answer to them. We have not had a very clear understanding about the efficient relationship between the saving work that God did in Jesus and the difference that work can make in our lives and in our world today.

The key to the answer of that question is to understand that the saving work God did in Jesus was a work of self-revelation. God acted in Jesus to make himself known. The God who made himself known through Jesus is still God today. The saving works that God did through Jesus are works that he is still doing today. If we can learn to recognize what God is doing in our world and in our lives and to be open and responsive to that work, God can do his saving work in and through our lives.

One of our problems is that most of us have lost any consciousness of God's presence in our lives. We have a way of thinking of God as being somewhere else, maybe somewhere on the other side of the sky. And our secularized culture has taught us that it a good thing to think like that. When we begin to think or talk about God doing anything in our lives, people are likely to give us funny looks and to think our capacity for rational thinking may have been impaired. But the angel who foretold the birth of Jesus said we would call him "Emmanuel, God is with us." (Matthew 1:23) Jesus has taught us that God is not somewhere else. God is with us.

But where and how is God with us? God is with us in all of our interactions with life. He is there in the touch of the hand of someone who loves you. He is there in the toast you eat for breakfast. He is there when your lives go through times of crisis. He is there when life makes demands upon you. He is there when life offers you new possibilities. He is there when a sunset moves you to hushed reverence. God comes to meet you in all of the different experiences of life. Your interactions with God work themselves out in your interactions with life. Life will be very different when you learn to think that God is always right there before you and beside you.

And, God is not only present in our lives and in our world today, God is active and at work in our lives and in our world today. No, that does not mean that God is causing everything that happens. God has decided not to do that. In the drama of life that swirls around us and that goes on within us, there are always currents and forces that work for good and others that work for harm. The ways in which they interact shape our lives and the course of human history. God is always at work in those forces that work to save us and our world from fear and greed and hate and the other things that would move us toward chaos. God is always at work in those forces that move us and our world toward fullness of life, the life of love.

But, how can we know which of the things that are going on in our lives and in our world are of God and which are not? Things can get awfully confusing in real life. God has made himself known through Jesus Christ so that we can recognize his work in our lives and in our world. The Bible writers have given us a story and stories that can help us know. The gospel writers have put together their accounts of the things that happened in the life of Jesus, the things he said, the things he did and the things that happened through him. They tell the story of the happening. And the different people who experienced life shaping interactions with God through Jesus have told us their stories of the things that happened to them so that we can know what can happen to us. We are going to spend a lot of time exploring that story and those stories.

Here is a key to what to expect. We can discover how Jesus can make a difference in our lives by doing three things. They will be our new three "Rs". Remember, Recognize, and Respond. Remember the things God did through Jesus. Recognize those things when we find them happening in our lives and in our world. Respond in ways that will allow God's saving work to be done in you and through you.

Prayer: Open my eyes so I can see.

The Story and the Stories

We can get in touch with God's self-revelation by reading the stories of Jesus from the Bible. There are two kinds of stories of Jesus in the Bible. There is the story of what actually happened in his life. Then there are many different stories of a different kind. They are stories that are like metaphors told by people who had life shaping experiences with Jesus and who are trying to tell us what God has done for them.

Matthew, Mark, Luke, and John have each given us their version of the story of Jesus. They tell us what happened, what Jesus said, what Jesus did, and what happened to him. They tell us the stories of the death and resurrection of Jesus and at least the beginning of the story of the ways in which the church prepared to carry on the work of Jesus after he died. (Luke writes a second volume in the form of the book of Acts that tells more about the follow through.) Luke tells us how he went about composing his books. He says he investigated everything very carefully from the beginning, especially the reports handed down from those who were eye witnesses and servants of the word, and then wrote an orderly account so that the readers can know the truth about the things that had happened. (Luke 1:1-4) He tells us that he did a research paper. The other three writers went about their work in a similar way. It is true that they were more interested in witnessing to the meaning of what happened and relating it to certain readerships than they were in writing a completely accurate historical account. That is why their books are called gospels instead of biographies. Even so, between them, they have given us a fairly reliable account of what happened in the life of Jesus. This is important. We need to know that story. It is the base line for our remembrance of Jesus. And it is important that it actually happened. The fact that it happened demonstrates that God has very intentionally acted in love to reach out to us and to make himself known to us and to make a difference in our lives and in the course of human history.

But there are other stories of a different kind. They are often more implied by figures of speech than actually told. Some are suggested by the names by which the early witnesses called Jesus. They are like parables or metaphors that the biblical witnesses used to tell us what God had done for them.

I had an experience early in my ministry that, I think, helped me to understand how that happened. My first appointment as a pastor was to a little church in a very rural part of Northeast Texas. There, the warm summer weeks after the farmers had ploughed their corn crops for the last time before harvest were revival time. The churches in the rural communities took turns holding week long programs of evangelistic preaching. The people met in the morning and in the evening for energetic services of singing and preaching. In the church I served, it was also a custom for people to meet for half an hour before the services started for "grove meetings". These were little groups of people who met in the groves of trees around the church building for prayer and sharing. Before one of our revival services, I found myself meeting with a group of men in clean denims for sharing.

The men gathered quietly. They were mostly naturally shy and unaccustomed to speaking in a group. The leader said, "Well, you know what we are here for. Does anyone want to say anything?" There was a long pause, the men looking down at the ground. Eventually, one man stirred, shuffled his feet, and said, "Well, I just want to say that the Lord has filled my cup." Everyone nodded appreciatively and went quiet again. Eventually another man spoke up and said, "Well you all know me. You know what my life was like. My life was on the trash heap. But God picked it up and cleaned it off and gave it back to me." Again the group nodded and went quiet. Finally another man spoke up and said, "Well, I just want to speak up and say which side I'm on."

These men were not repeating anything they had read or that they had been told. They were sharing their own experiences. They were using colorful language that suggested stories that described their personal experiences. The people who heard those witnesses appreciated them. They heard people whom they knew sharing something that was real. They were able to believe that, if that kind of thing could happen to their friends, something similar could happen to them. It was a powerful experience.

About dark thirty, the piano in the church house began to play and the people gathered into the building to sing songs and to hear preaching that was full of classical doctrinal language about atonement and reconciliation and redemption and to hear Jesus referred to as Savior and Messiah and Lord. As I have reflected on that experience, I have come to believe that all of those big ideas of the Christian faith may have started out as personal witnesses like those that were shared in the grove meeting. I believe that the people who first used ideas like atonement and reconciliation, and those who found so many expressive names to call Jesus were using colorful language to suggest stories that would tell us what God had done for them through Jesus.

The person who wrote the first epistle of John tells us "up front" that he is sharing something that is real to him because he has experienced it. He is sharing it in the hope that we may enter into his experience. "We declare to you what was from the beginning, what we have heard, what we have seen with our eyes, what we have looked on and touched with our hands, concerning the word of life—that life was revealed and we have seen it and testify to it, and declare to you the eternal life that was with the Father and was revealed to us—we declare to you what we have seen and heard so that you also may have fellowship with us: and truly, our fellowship is with the Father and with his son Jesus Christ. We are writing these things so that our joy may be complete." (1John 1:1-4) What he said about his writing, may very well apply to the work of many of the Bible writers.

In the reflections that follow, we are going to look at some of the most important names by which Jesus was called and think about what those names may suggest about what God had done in the lives of those who called Jesus by those names. It will be a fascinating study.

But it will be more than that. The stories of what God did in the lives of those biblical witnesses will suggest some of the things God may do in our own lives. The God who was at work in Jesus is still at work in our lives and in our world today. Do you remember the old gospel song that says, "It is no secret what God can do. What he's done for others, he can do for you." ?

We are going to discover that there is a fascinating variety of descriptions of the saving works of God. When God comes to us, he relates to us in terms of our own unique needs and possibilities. He does for us what we need to move us toward fullness of life. The variety of experiences that the biblical witnesses describe suggest a wide variety of possibilities that are there for us. We will find that they describe a wide variety of God's responses to human needs.

As we listen to the witnesses of the Bible writers, we will be prepared to apply the principle of the three "Rs". We will **remember** what the biblical witnesses say God has done for them. We will watch to **recognize** anything like that that may be happening in our lives or in our world. And we will be ready to **respond** in ways that will make it possible for God to do his saving work in us and through us.

Prayer: You are putting exciting possibilities into my life Lord. Help me be ready to respond.

The Savior Makes God Known

One of the most powerful biblical witnesses to the saving work of God has taught us to call Jesus "The Word." That suggests that God has something important to tell us and that he has chosen to speak through Jesus.

Every one of us has some assumptions or expectations that shape the ways in which we relate ourselves to life. When you walk out the door to go to work on Monday morning, what kind of expectations are at work in your life? Some people go to meet life thinking, "Well here comes another day of meaningless drudgery, something to be endured." Others walk out the door thinking, "This will be another venture into a hostile world, another fight for survival." Still others may think, "Here is another chance to grab all I can for myself." You can guess how each of those sets of expectations could shape a person's life.

But what if you could walk out the door thinking, "This day is a good gift from someone who loves me"? "I know everything may not go like I want it to and I know there will be challenges to be met, but I will not be alone in it. There will be someone there working with me. And, when the day is done, it will have been good." What would your life be like if you could really let those expectations shape your days? It becomes possible to go to meet life in that way when you know that the God who was made known to us in Jesus is coming to meet us in life. Being able to live in that way is part of what it means to be saved.

The first half of the first chapter of the gospel according to John is another of those great biblical prologues that summarizes the meaning of what is to follow. What is to follow is John's account of the story of the life of Jesus. The prologue tells us that, in Jesus, "The Word", an aspect of God's own being, "...became flesh and lived among us". (John 1:14) It also says, "No one has ever seen God. It is God the only Son, who is close to the Father's heart, who has made him known." (John 1:18) and "to all who received him, who believed in his name, he gave power to become children of God..." (John 1:12) That is one of the great biblical witness stories about how salvation happens.

The knowledge of God that Jesus brings is not just theological knowledge. It is not just information about some supernatural being who dwells in some remote heaven. Instead, it is a first hand experience of a greater reality who comes to meet us in every moment of our lives.

But how can that happen for us today. The thing that makes the saving work of Jesus work for us today is the knowledge that, what God did through Jesus so long ago, God is still doing in our lives and in our world today. If we can remember what God did then and recognize the times when God is doing it again now. Then we can respond in ways that will enable us to enter into life shaping relationships with the God who is still at work to save.

When and where can we experience God making God's self known to us today? When we ask that question, many people immediately begin to think of some exceptional experience like a narrow escape from an accident that they can think of as an intervention of God. That is probably not the best kind of example. It leaves us wondering why God did not intervene in all of the other situations in which we wanted a miracle.

I find myself experiencing the reality of God in the beauty and order of the natural world, in the wonder of the birth of a baby, and in the amazing fact that healing happens. I know that none of these things can be taken as scientific proof for the existence of God. But to me, they are demonstrations of the reality of God and they move me to awe. I know that many very sophisticated people have shared the same experience.

A young scientist once shared with me what he said was his most profound experience of God. He said it came while he was working with a research team trying to fill in one of the blank spots in humanity's understanding of the chemical elements. He said he was at the computer when the answer they had been seeking for months finally came together. He realized that he and his fellow scientists had been able to push back one of the limitations of human knowledge. To him, that was an experience of the order of the universe and of the reality of God.

I also experience the presence of love in the world as a revelation of the reality of God. I have said this before, love is not to be taken for granted. There is so much hate and indifference in the world that we might be tempted to think that those things are the natural order of things. But sometimes there is love, real love. And sometimes it happens in situations that make loving very difficult. When that happens, I believe that God must have been at work to make it happen.

Louie Armstrong used to sing a song in which he said: "I see friends greeting friends, saying "How do you do?" They're only saying, "I love you". And I say to myself, "What a wonderful world." To me, that is an affirmation of faith.

When have you experienced the reality of God? Can you see that experience as a time when God, The Word, has been at work in your life to save?

Prayer: Lord, teach me your new way of going to meet life.

The Savior Brings a New Possibility

Do you ever find yourself thinking that life is really not very good and that it is not likely to get any better? That is not a very good way to feel. In the time just before Jesus came, most of the Jewish people were feeling that way. They were politically oppressed and spiritually hungry. It was natural for them to remember the promises that the ancient prophets had made, the promise that God would send a messiah to save his people. That gave them a hope to hold on to, a hope for a new possibility.

Unfortunately, most of the people hoped for a messiah who would be a military leader who would drive out the Roman army of occupation and end the political oppression. I suppose it is natural for us to think first about changes we would like to have made in our circumstances.

But the prophets' promise had another dimension. The prophets promised a new king who would come and reorganize the life of the nation and of the people around a new center, a center in God. He would teach them to put their trust in the power and in the love of God. He would teach them to live in obedience to the will and purpose of God. That would indeed bring a new possibility, even if the circumstances could not be changed. But the new possibility would be a new kind of life that would eventually change even the circumstances.

Jesus came bringing that second kind of new possibility. He came preaching, "The time is fulfilled, and the kingdom of God has come near, repent and believe the good news." (Mark 1:15) Some of those whose lives were changed by their interactions with Jesus told a story about a new king coming. He came to set people free from both outer and inner oppression. He came to teach a new way of life centered in

God, a way in which God is the most important thing, the king. That is one of the great witness stories that describe the saving work of God. Eventually, Jesus came to be recognized as the Messiah or the Christ, the bringer of the new possibility.

Do we need a new possibility? Is everything really as it should be in our lives and in our world? How have we been taught to put our lives together? How is life in our world put together? Isn't it most often organized around the pursuit of material wealth? Aren't we taught by our culture to put our trust in wealth and to organize our lives around getting wealth and managing it? Aren't we taught to evaluate everything, even ourselves, in terms of how many dollars they are worth?

How is that working for us? Many of us are so caught up in that way of life that we think it is really all that we could want our lives to be. But what happens when the economy goes sour and we find ourselves moving down the ladder of affluence instead of up? Is it just a practical problem that we have to cope with? Or is it a spiritual crisis that has us feeling like failures and asking questions about the meaning of life? Would we really be free to decide to live on less if there were a good reason to, or are we addicted to our prosperity?

How is this way of putting life together working for our world? Has it indeed provided well being for all of the people of the world? Or are great portions of the population of the world living in desperate poverty while wealth accumulates in the hands of` a powerful few? Could that be the real cause of the frustration and hate that threatens the world with destructive conflict?

Reckoning with these very real realities might enable us to hear God saying to us again what he said long ago in the words of Jesus, "It is time for a change. Dare to believe that there is a better possibility. And be ready to make the changes necessary to cause it to happen."

What might life be like if we allowed ourselves to take seriously the things that Jesus taught in the Sermon on the Mount? (Matthew 5-7). Remember: "Do not worry saying 'What shall we eat?' or 'What shall we drink?' or 'What shall we wear?' … Your Father knows you need all of these things. But strive first for the kingdom of God and his righteousness, and all of these things will be given to you as well."

(Matthew 6: 31-33) And, "In everything do to others as you would have them do to you…" (Matthew 7; 12).

What might it be like to live according to the way of love that Jesus taught? What would it be like to believe that the most real of all realities is not all of the money in all of the banks of the world but rather the God who was made known through Jesus Christ? How would it be if we evaluated ourselves and others, not in terms of how much money we have accumulated, but rather in terms of the value God attributes to us by loving us? And what might this world look like if we should learn to love our neighbors so that we are committed to the well being of all people and not just to our own advantage? It stretches our minds to think about it. But it really would be a new possibility, wouldn't it?

It may seem a bit much to think about changing the whole world at one time. But we should know that the new possibility that God offers to us is something into which we can enter one person at a time. You can choose to let your own life be reorganized around the reality of God. Your friends will probably think of you as someone who marches to the beat of a different drummer. But you can enjoy the liberation that comes from trusting God and the meaning that comes from being committed to the purpose of God. You can know that new quality of life that is the life of the kingdom. You may become an agent of God's new possibility.

There is a story from recent world history that demonstrates what it can mean to claim a new possibility. During the last years of Communism in Poland, many of the people began to yearn for a life of freedom. The members of the Solidarity movement decided upon a strategy. People said to one another, "Start doing the things that ought to be done and start being what you think society ought to become. If you believe in free speech, speak freely. If you believe in the truth, tell it. If you believe in an open society, then act in the open." The behavior caught on. By acting as if Poland were already a free country, Solidarity created a free country. It took great courage to do that in a country with a Communist regime and governed by marshal law. But it worked. Within ten years, Solidarity had taken over the government. (Walter Wink. *Engaging the Powers*, Minneapolis, Fortress Press, 1992, P. 265)" By choosing the new possibility for yourself and living in it, you can claim a new life for yourself and you may even be able to change the world.

Jesus came to bring a new possibility. Are you ready for it? Are you ready to believe that the time has indeed come? Are you ready to repent, that is, to make the needed changes in your life and to believe that the coming of that new possibility really is good news?

Prayer: You really are asking us to look at everything in a different way, aren't you Lord?

The Savior Confronts Us with Our Needs

What does it take to get your attention? A mechanic tells you that one of your tires is about to blow out and, if it happens while you are traveling at a high speed, it could cause a dangerous accident. A doctor tells you that you have a melanoma and that it needs attention right away. Your teenager is begins to act out in ways that let you know that all is not well in your home life. Your boss and your spouse tell you that, unless you get your drinking under control, you will lose your job and your marriage. A racial conflict occurs that lets your community know that, unless some changes are made, something really destructive could happen. All of these are crisis situations that can tell you that something is wrong and some changes need to be made.

In the popular religion of the Jewish people in the time just before Jesus began his ministry, there was an expectation that God would send an agent of judgment and warning to perform a similar function. These people believed that the world as they knew it was about to come to an end and that there would be a day of judgment on which everyone living would be consigned either to heaven or to hell. They believed that, just before that day, God would send a special representative to warn the people and to call them to make needed changes before it was too late. This story of the coming of an agent of warning was one of the stories that some of the biblical witnesses borrowed to tell about the saving work that God had done in their lives.

Scholars have a hard time understanding all that is said about that agent of change. Some of the biblical witnesses refer to that coming one as "the prophet of the last days." Others refer to him as "The Son of Man".

Now, here is something interesting. In the Bible, we hear different witnesses calling Jesus by many different names, each of which suggests some saving work of God. But the name by which Jesus most often referred to himself is "The Son of Man." Could it be that Jesus understood it to be his mission to warn people that everything was not okay in their lives and in their world, to offer them a better possibility, and to call them to make needed changes before it was too late? That could have certainly been a part of his purpose when he came preaching, "…the kingdom of God has come near. Repent and believe the good news."(Mark 1:15)

The Bible tells many stories of Jesus doing things that were meant to fulfill that function. He told a respected old Pharisee named Nicodemus that he needed to start all over and put his life together in an entirely different way. He said, "You must be born from above". (John 3:1-21) He told a young man whose wealth was too important to him that he needed to give all of his wealth to charity and to come and become one of his disciples. (Mark 10:17-31) And he pushed himself into the life of his people in a way that required them to choose between the way of love that he was teaching and the way of hate that they were following. (Mark 15:1-15) The people did not always make the right decisions. But many who met Jesus were confronted with their needs.

When we come into interaction with the risen Christ today, we are often confronted with our needs and our need to make important decisions. Evangelistic preachers often called people to "make a decision for Christ" at the end of revival services in churches. But I wonder if Christ is not coming to meet us again and again in all of the crisis situations of our lives and forcing us to reckon with the fact that everything is not okay. I wonder if he comes in all of those situations to offer us a better possibility and to require us to make a decision. I wonder if he comes to confront communities and nations and the whole human race in those times when greed and hate are doing their destructive work. I wonder if he comes then offering us the real possibility of a life shaped by love and requiring us to make an important decision.

What might this kind of confrontation look like in our own

personal lives? Let's try this. (This may not work for you, but then, it may.) Call to mind the last crisis situation in your life when something really important had to change. If things had gone on as they had been, something bad would have happened. Were you required to make a decision about that change? Were any of the alternatives open to you something that could have represented an aspect of God's new possibility? Or, was the situation such that it was good news just to realize that there was another possibility open to you?

Maybe you can remember a situation in the life of a friend or a family member that demanded some attention, some decision, some change of direction. Did you feel that you needed to call that crisis to the attention of your friend? Can you visualize the ways in which God's saving work might have been going on in that situation?

Prayer: Lord, I really don't like those crisis confrontations. Is it really you who are pushing us into them?

The sun barely peeked above the horizon,

When I boarded the Boliver Ferry.

But, before the short ride was over,

It hung full and round above the water.

I had never realized before,

How fast the sun rises,

How fast the world turns,

How fast my life passes.

I do not have a moment to waste.

The Savior Forgives and Accepts

It is as if I had been put on trial for all of the wrongness in my life and found guilty. My wrongness was costly because it was destructive to my life and to the lives of others and to life in God's creation. I was sentenced to die and to suffer eternal punishment for my guilt. But another person, who had no guilt or wrongness, came and died in my place. He absorbed the cost and paid the penalty for my wrongness so that I could be freely given the status of a just person and a beloved child of God.

That is a summary of one of the best known and most important of the biblical witness stories. It is a story told by people who wanted to witness to the forgiving and accepting love of God. The story is not actually told in exactly that way anywhere in the Bible. But it is implied in many places. Some of them are: Romans 3:21-26, Romans 5:6-11, Hebrews 2:17-18, Hebrews 10:10, and 1John 4:10. It is probably the most important theme in the witness of Paul.

Unfortunately, down through the ages of the history of the church, many people have treated this story as if it were the whole story of salvation. It is not. Guilt is only one of the things that separate us from God and from fullness of life. But we all have to reckon with it. It is one of the things from which we all need to be saved. We all need to hear the good news of God's forgiving and accepting love.

It is important for us to realize that this story is a parable that witnesses to one aspect of God's saving work, not a description of a historical event. If we miss that, we may get lost in questions about why God required someone to die before he would forgive. Those questions have to do with the stage settings of the drama. The point of the story is that God forgives our wrongness. God sets our guilt aside so that we can be free from it, so that we can know that God loves us in spite of our wrongness, and so that we can make a fresh start.

The story of the suffering of Christ makes it clear that this forgiving is not a thing that can be done lightly. Our wrongness has done serious harm that has to be absorbed before we can be forgiven. The image of Jesus suffering on the cross provides a vivid picture of God, and of all humanity, and of the whole creation, having to suffer the results of our wrongness and to absorb them so that we can be free to live.

Can you take in what that can mean to you? There are two kinds of people who will find this witness most meaningful.

One is the kind of person who feels that he has been measured, found lacking, and rejected. This can happen in many different circumstances in life, both religious and secular. Those who feel that they have been rejected and condemned to be outsiders can rejoice in the knowledge that they have been accepted into the love of God and given the possibility of fullness of life.

The other people who can find this witness most meaningful are those who are oppressed by the knowledge that they have done something really wrong, something that has caused suffering for others or for humanity as a whole. Maybe it was a crime, or a lie, or an unfaithfulness, or something done during a war.

You have to fill in the blank here. Is there something in your life that you regret so deeply that it is inhibiting your ability to go to meet life as a whole person?

This witness brings the good news that the cost of your wrongness has been absorbed and set aside. That can be a real liberation. This liberation is there for you. You may still have to reckon with the results of your wrongness. Knowing that you are loved in spite of everything that is wrong in your life, loved by the one who really counts, can restore your personhood. But, it is important to remember that receiving God's forgiving and accepting love is the beginning of the process of being saved, not the end of it.

There are two questions that you can ask that will bring belief in the atonement to life in your experience. First, when and where do you experience God's forgiving and accepting love in your own relationships with life and with others? Second, when and where does love require you to absorb the cost of the wrongness of others so that you can accept them and help them to enter into God's new possibility?

Prayer: Now, Lord, you are pushing into the parts of my live that I would like to keep secret. Do I dare to believe your promise to forgive strongly enough to let you in?

The Savior Liberates.

At the time when this is being written, the people of Libya are celebrating their liberation from an oppressive government. They have lived for decades under a regime that has restricted the freedom of the people and of the nation to become all that they can become. Now they hope to be free and to move toward a better possibility.

There is a theme in the New Testament that compares the saving work of God to that kind of liberation. The Bible writers tell two stories that suggest that.

Some call Jesus the redeemer. That suggests a story in which someone has either been sold into slavery or put into debtor's prison. But a friend comes, either to pay the debt or to buy the slave out of bondage and to set him free. Some passages of scripture that suggest this are Ephesians 1:3-14 and Galatians 5:1.

The other liberation story suggests that a person—or the whole human race—is living under the reign of an oppressor who is the devil. But Jesus came, according to the custom of ancient warfare, to be the champion who would engage the enemy in single combat and defeat him so that the people could go free. People who tell this story often refer to Jesus as the victor. Some passages that suggest this story are: 1Corinthians 15:50-58, Hebrews 2:14-15, Romans 8:31-39, and the book of Revelation.

Oppression can take many forms in our lives. There are still millions of people who are living under political oppression. People are still being sold into slavery. An abusive family situation can be a form of oppression. So can an addiction. Some people sell themselves into oppression through obsessive ambitions. Any time a person, or a group of people, is kept from moving toward full humanity by some force, either within themselves or without, there is oppression. Every external oppressor must have a collaborator within the person or the people who are oppressed. Every threat must relate to some fear. Every temptation must relate to some desire.

God created us to be free and responsible people and communities and to use our freedom to let our lives be shaped by our interactions with God.

Unfortunately, many people think that freedom means permission to be irresponsible. That is certainly not what God has in mind. God wants us to be free to learn the life of love for which we were created.

The Bible tells us a story in which Jesus claimed his freedom and used it to live in the service of the purpose of God. This is one of those aspects of the story of the saving work of God that makes it important to remember that Jesus was human just as we are. He was subject to the same temptations and threats that come to bear upon our lives, and he had to make human decisions just like we do. Temptations and threats and all of the powerful forces at work in his world worked to turn him aside from the commitment he had made. But he would not be turned aside. In doing that, Jesus has shown us the shape of freedom and he has also demonstrated that we can live freely. (We will say more about that later) His death upon the cross was a victory for humanity, a refusal to let even the threat of death turn him aside. His resurrection was a victory of God over death.

It takes great courage to claim freedom and to live beyond the control of the threats and the enticements and the powers that would oppress us. Sometimes we have to claim our freedom to live as whole persons even when we have to keep on living under circumstances that would oppress us. Sometimes claiming freedom can actually eventually change the circumstances that oppress. Remember the story of the Solidarity movement in Poland. Sometimes a person can claim freedom by simply deciding to keep oppression external to himself or herself. A person with a family to support may have to keep working under an abusive employer, at least until he of she can find a better job. But the employee can refuse to let the abuse define his or her personhood.

Liberation can happen in the lives of persons, communities, or nations. God gives us our freedom. Christ has demonstrated what it means to live as free people and calls us to follow him in doing it. Then, God calls us to become agents of liberation in the world. When we learn to love as God loves, we will want to work for the liberation of those whom we love. Think hard about what that means. We may think we know what is good for those whom we love and we may be working hard to help that happen for them. But we must remember to do that in the ways that God does it, ways that respect the freedom of those we are trying to lead. That same thing must be true in the relationships between groups and nations. We must want and respect the freedom of others, even while we are working for their good. When we see another living in an oppressive situation, as in an abusive family relationship, we may want to urge that one to claim freedom, but we must be very aware that there may be a great cost involved in doing that. This can make the work of loving both difficult and costly.

When I think of this witness to the saving work of God I often think of Alan, a young man who came and joined our church while he was on parole, awaiting trial for a violent crime committed against another person while he was under the influence of drugs. When he told me his story, I think he expected me to tell him to go away. Instead, I told him that, if he was serious about getting his life together with the help of the Christian faith, I really wanted him to stay. He stayed. I worked with him as he began his spiritual pilgrimage. But too soon, he was brought to trial and found guilty—because he was. I urged him to continue his quest for wholeness through the prison chapel. He did. We corresponded occasionally. Eventually he wrote to tell me that the chaplain had asked him to give a personal witness during the chapel service. He sent me a copy of the talk he was about to make. The main theme of the witness was that God had set him free, free from his guilt and free from the compulsions that caused his crime. He said that, even though he had to stay behind the prison walls to serve out his sentence, he was free.

In time, I lost contact with Alan. I often wondered about him. Then one day I found his parents address among some old papers. I wrote to them asking about him. Soon I got a letter from Alan himself. He said, "I am one of those for whom it worked. I am married. I have a daughter. I have my own business. We are in church every Sunday." He was indeed free.

Prayer: We talk a lot about freedom, Lord. But it is really a frightening thing. Give me the courage to claim freedom and to live it.

The Savior Calls Us
To High Purpose

I once had the privilege of serving a church near the National Aeronautics and Space Administration Center in Houston. Many of the people in the church were among those who first put American astronauts into space. One of the astronauts was a member of the church while I served it. It was exciting to be around those people because they all shared a sense of being committed to a very special purpose. Each person who played any role in the preparation and completion of one of the missions was given a plaque with a copy of the mission insignia on it. They displayed those trophies proudly in their homes. It was obvious that they had gotten great satisfaction out of having been a part of something really big and important. Having a purpose big enough to be worth living for adds an important dimension to any person's life. .

It's personal witness time. I believe that one of the biggest gifts that the Christian faith has given to me is a purpose big enough to be worth living for. That is something I need. I honestly believe that the faith the Christian church teaches is the hope of the world. Please understand that I am talking about the way of love that the Christian faith teaches and enables. I believe that it is the hope for wholeness for every person. It is the way to the really good life. And I believe it is the hope of the whole world for peace, justice and well being for all people. There are lots of ways in which people can serve that purpose. I have served it quite intentionally through the ministry of the church. Yes, I know about the church's failures. I know better than most. And I have experienced many disappointments. But, as I approach the end of my life, I find great satisfaction in believing that I have spent my life doing something really important.

Bible scholars tell us that Jesus probably made a decision early in his life to serve the purpose of God.

There was a belief among the people of Israel that God sought special people who would commit themselves wholly and unconditionally to serve the purpose of God. God could work through these people in special ways to accomplish his purpose on earth. These people were known as the "ebed Jahweh", or servant of God. Those who committed themselves to God in that way would have to expect that their service would involve suffering. The most vivid image of the suffering servant of God is to be found in Isaiah 52:13-53:12. You may recognize some of the words from that passage. "He was despised and rejected by others, a man of suffering and acquainted with infirmity…", "He was wounded for our transgressions, crushed for our iniquities; upon him was the punishment that made us whole…"

It seems likely that Jesus knew that tradition and that he came to believe that God had called him to play the role of the servant of God. He made a courageous human decision to respond to that calling. In this, we see the coming together of the purpose of the eternal God and a commitment made by a human being like ourselves. That commitment was dramatized when Jesus came to his cousin, John the Baptist, to be baptized in the Jordan River. (Matthew 3:13-17) That coming together of the purpose of God and the commitment of the man, Jesus, continued to shape everything that Jesus did. The life of Jesus became the pivotal act of God for the salvation of the world.

Soon after Jesus began his ministry, he began to approach others and to say, "Follow me." (Matthew 4:18-22) He was calling others to commit themselves to the same purpose that was shaping his life. He calls us too. Ultimately, the life he calls us to is the life of love, a joyful commitment of life to life. It can be costly, but it is also deeply satisfying and truly joyful. The gift of a purpose big enough to be worth living for is one of the most precious gifts of God and one of the most important saving works of God.

What are you living for? The purpose of God is there for you. I have served it as a pastor but goodness knows that is not the only way to serve it. The clergy are just the facilitators. The salvation of the world really comes when home makers and teachers and carpenters and industrial workers and engineers and financiers and business people and politicians and all of the other people who are involved in making the world work decide to organize their lives in ways that serve the loving purpose of God. The call of Christ is most likely to come to you as you are thinking seriously about all of the things you see going on in the world around you—and all of the needs that could be met—and all of the things that need to be fixed. The call may beckon you to leave the place where you are and to venture out into some new and distant endeavor. But it is more likely to call you to reorganize all of the things you are doing right now around God's loving purpose.

When I think about the purpose of God I often think of a brief poem that came out of the trauma of the Second World War. I do not know who wrote it but I remember what it said. A group of Christian leaders were meeting during the early days of the war and someone brought to the group the sad news that her city of Shanghai China was being bombed. Soon after that, someone in the group wrote these words: "Tonight Shanghai is burning/ And we are dying too/ For there is no death so complete,/ As the death inside of you./ For some men die by shrapnel/ And some go down in flames/ While other men just waste away/ And play at little games.

What are you living for?

Prayer: Lord, help me to discover a purpose for my life that is big enough to be worth living for.

The Savior is Someone to Follow

If a preacher stands up in a pulpit and tells people to claim their freedom, to commit themselves to the purpose of God, and to live the life of love, someone is bound to respond: "That all sounds good but it is not realistic. No one with human limitations like ours can live that kind of life in the real world where we live." The biblical witnesses answer, "Someone has done it. A real man, having limitations like yours, living under circumstances like yours or worse, has indeed lived that life to show us how to do it, to show us that it can be done, and to call us to follow him. His name was Jesus."

Late in the time when the Bible was being written, the writer of the book of Hebrews gathered up several of the most important witnesses to the saving work of God and wove them together into a story intended to make clear the meaning of the story of the life of Christ that was told by the gospel writers. The book of Hebrews is hard to understand. But if you gaze at it long enough, a story line will emerge like the figures hidden in one of those "magic eye" pictures. We are going to wade through parts of the book of Hebrews to see how that story takes shape. We will learn what it means to call Jesus "The Pioneer of our faith".

The writer starts by assuring us that the main actor in this narrative is God. The one who becomes the protagonist in this story is an aspect of God's own being. (Hebrews 1:1-4) Then the writer tells us that this one came to live among us as one who was in every way human, just as we are. He came to experience life—and death—just as we experience it. (Hebrews 2:9-11)

The incarnation means that God has come to identify with us and to share life with us. Jesus came to live among us as a brother and to regard us as his brothers and sisters. (Hebrews 2:11-13) Can you take in the meaning of that? Can you see what value God attributes to you? Can you see what importance God attributes to your life and to the things going on in the world in which you live?

The incarnation means that God actually became vulnerable for our sake. He left the security of "Heaven" and of omnipotence to become vulnerable to suffering and to all of the uncertainties of life as we live it. (Hebrews 1:3) The incarnation means that God has joined us in our suffering. (Hebrews 2:9)

God became human in order to help us become divine. That idea throws us a curve doesn't it? Yet, it was a very important concept in the theology of the early church. What does it mean? It does not mean that God is going to do some magic to change us from human beings into gods. It means that Jesus came to help us recover the image of God within us and to live up to our highest God given possibilities, to live truly human lives, to love like God loves.

The book of Hebrews tells us that the incarnation positioned Jesus to do two of the saving works that we have mentioned earlier. He made atonement for our sins. (Hebrews 2:17) and he defeated the powers of death. (Hebrews 2:14-15)

With those obstacles out of the way, Jesus went on to live an example of the truly human life for which we were created. Having entered into humanity like ours and having become subject to all of the conditions of our human lives, he lived a life that was in every way like ours but without sin. (Hebrews 4:15) The story of the life of Jesus that we read in the four gospels is a story of a man whose life was shaped by a perfect relationship with God. He lived a life of trust and of love. He lived human life at its best. "Although he was a son, he learned obedience through what he suffered; and having been made perfect, he became the source of eternal salvation for those who obey him." (Hebrews 5:7-9)

The book of Hebrews then goes on to tell us of another ministry of Jesus. After the resurrection, he became an enabler for those who try to follow Jesus the pioneer. We will think about that in a reflection called, "A Friend by our side."

Near the end of the book of Hebrews, the writer addresses a calling to us. "…let us lay aside every weight and the sin that clings so closely and let us run with perseverance the race that is set before us, looking to Jesus, the pioneer and perfecter of our faith, who for the sake of the joy that was set before him, endured the cross, disregarding the shame, and has taken his seat at the right hand of the throne of God." (Hebrews 12:1-2)

The book of Hebrews tells a story that makes me think of a track coach who comes to a defeated and demoralized team to show them how to run an obstacle course. First he tells them how to do it. Then he runs the course himself to show them how to do it and to show them that it can be done. Then he stands at the finish line shouting to the team members, "Come on! If I can do it, you can do it. Come on and be a winner."

It is important for us to be able to recognize the ways in which God does that saving work in our lives so that we can experience it today. We will talk about that next.

Prayer: I just don't know about that, Lord. You are taking away my excuses.

The Savior is The Pioneer Next Door

It has been very meaningful for me to think of Jesus as the pioneer of our faith. The book of Hebrews tells us that, in Jesus, an aspect of God's own being entered our life situation to live among us as one of us to show us that we can live the life for which God created us under our own real world circumstances. (Hebrews 2:10-18) Having been taught to look for God working in that way, I have often seen God working through other people, every day people whom I knew—or of whom I knew—who have demonstrated that high possibility by living up to their own highest humanity in this real world.

Of course I am inspired by the great heroes of the faith like Mother Teresa and Desmond Tutu. But I am even more inspired by the people I find living out an example of fullness of life right next door. I am still inspired by the little hunch backed lady who shared her high culture by taking a magnifying glass and books from the church library and walking around the small town where she lived to read to the shut ins, some of whom were younger than she. I still hold in high regard the retired engineer who organized a group of his friends to build wheel chair ramps for people who needed them but could not afford them. .When you look for people who can play the role of the pioneer for you, don't look for perfection. There is very little of that around. But if you look for genuine goodness, you will find more of that than you expect, and you will find it in unexpected places.

The one who stands the tallest among my heroes of the faith is a little man named Bonito. He was the patriarch of the first Hispanic family that moved into the previously all Anglo community where I grew up. Most of the people who remained in the old neighborhood were older people who could remember when their community was a nicer place to live. Many of the houses in the neighborhood had been allowed to run down. The two old houses right across the street from my mother's house had been abandoned. The paint was peeling. The windows were broken. The yards were full of weeds. Then the first Hispanic family moved in, three generations at once. They occupied the two old houses across the street. Needless to say, apprehension was high. Would this be the last straw that would break the community.

But the first surprises were good ones. Bonito and his family undertook to clean up the old houses. The neighbors watched as the weeds disappeared, the windows were repaired, and fresh white paint replaced the dingy grey. Beside that, Bonito became a good neighbor to everyone. He hired himself out to do home repairs at a reasonable rate. Bonito's married daughter and her family rented my mother's upstairs apartment. The neighborhood became a happier place.

But eventually another group of new neighbors moved in, the kind that the neighborhood had been fearing. They were a group of sullen young people who seemed to be always hanging around the old house they rented at the time when they might have been expected to be at work. In fact, they turned out to be members of a criminal gang.

Because the newcomers were Hispanic, Bonito seemed to feel responsible for representing the neighborhood to them. He tried to talk to them about the things that worried the neighbors but it was evident that they were paying him no attention. Things were not good.

Then one afternoon, while Bonito was visiting his daughter on my mother's upstairs front porch, he saw a frightening drama being played out. An old Anglo man from down the street walked by on the way to the corner grocery store. He was obviously drunk. As he returned from the store, he passed the house where the young people lived. They came out and stopped him and took his cigarettes out of his grocery sack. A loud confrontation followed. Boneto and his daughter watched. The old man went on home, cursing all of the way. In a few minutes, he came back with an old single shot shotgun. He aimed it in the direction of the boys and fired it.

Bonito knew what was about to happen—and he must have known what could happen. The boys came running toward the old man. Bonito ran down the stairs and went to try to intercede. His daughter was shouting after him to come back. But he did not come back. He put himself between the boys and the old man. The boys turned their anger on Bonito. They had knives. They stabbed Bonito to death. There were more than thirty wounds on his body. Then they went away. Bonito's daughter cradled her father in her arms as he died. The police came and took the gang members away. The neighborhood was quiet again—but at what a great cost.

Every time I think of Bonito's heroism, I think I have heard of a repetition of the passion of Christ. I give thanks that tyranny will never rule completely so long as there are people like Bonito who will stand up to its threats. And I pray that, when the time comes for it, I will have the courage to live up to the highest that I know just as Bonito did.

Prayer: Thank you for people who live lives that show me my own best possibility.

The Savior is A Friend by Our Side

The book of Hebrews invites us to venture out into life as a follower of Jesus, the pioneer of out faith. (Hebrews 12:1-2) That invitation is exciting—challenging—frightening—overwhelming. We wonder what would be required, what would we be up against? Here is an invitation to "come to the edge" if there ever was one. We may find ourselves backing away from accepting that invitation. But wait. There is a promise that goes with the invitation. That makes accepting the invitation a much more real possibility for us.

The promise too comes from the book of Hebrews. But we may have to listen carefully to hear it.

The book of Hebrews tells us that God sent one who was an aspect of his own being to live among us as one of us, to identify with us, to claim us as members of his family. He came to experience life just as we experience it; hardships, temptations, suffering and all. Living under circumstances like ours, Jesus lived the life of love for which we were created. He did that to show us how to do it and to show us that it actually can be done. In these ways, Jesus acted as the pioneer of our faith, the one who goes before us and whom we should follow.

Then the book tells us that Jesus moved to another aspect of the saving work of God. Having accomplished his work among us, he went back to being an aspect of the reality of God. The book uses several images to tell us about that. It speaks of Jesus sitting at the right hand of God. It also speaks of Jesus representing us before God as a priest in a great heavenly temple, accomplishing the forgiving of our sins and being our advocate with the Father. In other words, there is someone there in the presence of God who understands what we are going through because he has been through it himself. There is someone there who is for us. That is good to know, isn't it?

But there may be even more to it than that. Where is this "heaven" in which Jesus represents us before God? We used to think of heaven as being somewhere on the other side of the sky, but we know better than that now. Isn't heaven where God is? And isn't God everywhere? Can we visualize heaven and all of the things that heaven is supposed to represent as being another dimension of the same reality that surrounds us right where we are? Apparently the writer of the book of Hebrews thought in those terms because he spoke of all of the people of faith who have gone to be with God as a great cloud of witnesses that stand around us. (Hebrews 11:1-12:2) So we can think of Jesus, the one who once came to live among us as still being here with us. That idea also shows up in other parts of the New Testament" Matthew 1:23, Matthew 28:20, John 14; 18-27.

So God is with us as we live our lives in this world. He comes to meet us in each new experience of life. He is always reaching out to us to do whatever is needed for our salvation. God is with us as the God of high expectations, the pioneer who goes before us living the life for which we were created. Even under difficult circumstances, he confronts us and calls us to take courage and follow.

But he is also the friend who walks by our side all of the way, one who understands, one who loves us as we are, one who is there to help us up when we fall, one who makes possible all that life and God require of us.

The writer of the book of Hebrews sums it up like this: "Since then we have a great high priest who has passed through the heavens, Jesus, the Son of God, let us hold fast to our confession. For we do not have a high priest who is unable to sympathize with our weakness, but one who in every respect has been tested as we are, yet without sin. Let us therefore approach the throne of grace with boldness, so that we may receive mercy and find grace to help in every time of need." (Hebrews 4:14-16) This is an invitation to venture out into life knowing that we have a friend who walks by our side.

How has this assurance been mediated to you through the experiences of your life? We have invited you to remember those who have represented God's high expectations to you. Now remember those who have mediated God's enabling grace to you. Who are those who have walked by your side, parents, mentors, marriage partners, friends? Have there been those who have been there to care, to accept, to help, to enable? If there have been such people, the Bible invites us to recognize them as "God with us".

Late one night while I was involved in editing these pages, I happened to flip the computer to this reflection and I realized what had just happened to me. My wife and I had just come from an appointment with my oncologist. He had just told us that my chemotherapy was not working. My time was limited. We both felt cheated because we had a beautiful marriage that had just lasted a little ore than a year. We had hoped to grow old together. We spent a long time standing in the kitchen sharing our deepest feelings. She assured me that she would be by my side to take care of me all of the way. She knew what she was promising. She had been through it before. I know God is by my side.

Even if there have not been such people, the gospel invites to imagine that there is one there who is an invisible presence by our side trying both to lead and to enable, a friend who is always there, indeed, God with us.

Prayer: Thanks, Lord. That helps.

An Affirmation
That Requires Commitment

Once I saw a person wearing a Tee shirt with these words printed on it, "Jesus Christ is Lord." I wonder if that person realized that those words represented the first great affirmation of faith of the early church. To say those words and mean them requires a commitment.

We have been reflecting on the names by which Jesus was called by the biblical witnesses. We have thought about what it means that the witnesses called Jesus names like: Word, Messiah, Son of Man, Atonement, Pioneer and High Priest. Most of those names were meant to call our attention to the saving works that God did through Jesus and is still doing in our lives and in our world today. It is important for us to be able to recognize the saving works that God does so that, when we encounter them in our lives, we can recognize them and open ourselves to the possibility they represent. But there are two names by which Jesus was called that go beyond making such a witness. They require us to make a decision about whether or not we will enter into that new possibility. Those names are "Lord" and "Savior".

These are the two names by which Jesus was known after the resurrection. Both are names by which the Jewish people were accustomed to referring to God. It is true that the title, "lord" could be used just as a term of respect, like "sir". No doubt, Jesus was often addressed in that way during his life and ministry. But after the resurrection, the name took on a bigger meaning. The believers realized that Jesus had not been just another great teacher or leader. They realized that he had represented God's presence among them. They also realized that he is not gone as other people who have died are gone. God is still alive and at work among us and so is that one who came from God and now has returned to being an aspect of the reality of God. They called Jesus "Lord" in recognition that he was—and still is—the presence of the living God among us.

What can it mean for us to call Jesus "Lord"? It must mean that we believe he really does represent that great other who comes to meet us in every moment of our lives. To call Jesus "Lord" must mean that we believe what he represents to us is the truth about all reality. It is to say we believe there really is a great other out there relating to us in all of the interactions of our lives. And it is to say we believe that great other really is as Jesus has represented him to be, one who is alive, active, intentional, loving, and at work to save. To call Jesus "Lord" is to adopt a whole new way of understanding life and of relating to it. That is one of the biggest decisions that any of us can make.

That leads us to the second aspect of what it means to call Jesus "Lord". To decide to do that is to decide to choose Jesus as the Lord of your life. A lord is a king. In biblical days, a king was the most important person in a realm, the one upon whom everything depended, the one whose will and purpose were obeyed. To call Jesus "Lord" is not only to say that Jesus and all that he represents are the most important of all realities but also to say that you have chosen to let Jesus and all that he represents be the most important reality in your life and to organize your life around him.

To make that decision will require courage and commitment. There will be no real conflict between a commitment to Jesus and a commitment to yourself and to those whom you love. What God wants for us is really what is best for us all. Loving God will lead us into a more perfect love for ourselves and for others. But it is likely to put us into conflict with our culture and with others who will have different ideas about what is important. In the early church, to call Jesus Lord was to say that he and not Caesar was the real king of their lives. That sometimes got them in trouble. It could get us into similar kinds of trouble. But putting the real first things first can give great integrity and vitality to our lives.

To decide to take Jesus as your savior requires a similar commitment. We have talked a lot about the ways in which Jesus shows us that God is at work to save. To take Jesus as our savior is to decide to let that happen in our lives.

First, we have to decide whether or not we really want to be saved. Many of us have gotten accustomed to the idea that the question, "Do you want to be saved?" means "Do you want to go to heaven when you die?" In the Bible, that question came closer to meaning, "Do you want to be made whole here and now?" We have to decide whether the wholeness that Jesus offers us is really what we want. That wholeness is a life shaped by love. Let's face it, some of us have some other ambitions to which we are pretty well committed. And some of the things from which God wants to save us may be things to which we have some attachment. It will take some doing for some of us to really come to believe that the life in which Jesus Christ is Lord is the very best life we could ever hope for.

Then being saved is a life long process of becoming. It is not some simple transaction that can be taken care of once and for all in a few minutes at the front of a church or in a brief conversation with an evangelist. You may announce your decision to begin the process in a setting like that and that can be a good thing to do. But being made whole is a matter of moving into life asking of each new interaction with life, "What is God trying to do in my life right now and how can I best respond so that it can happen?" That will mean that you will live in a constant process of letting your life be reshaped by your relationship with God. That will certainly turn your life into a new kind of adventure. But to live in that adventure is to really live.

To choose to let Jesus Christ be your Lord and Savior will require of you the biggest commitment of your life. But it will be a commitment that leads to real life.

Prayer: Help me to really want to call you "Lord" and "Savior".

Finding the Way Into A Personal Relationship With God

Reflections on the Witness of Paul, Romans 8

Are You Up For an Adventure?

To accept Jesus Christ as your Lord and savior is to begin an adventure in which you allow your life to be reshaped by your relationship with God. Now it's time to talk about that adventure.

When I look back over what I have written so far, I find that my focus has been mostly on things that God is doing. Now it seems appropriate for me to get around to the subjective side of religion. I need to write something about what it is like to live in a life shaping relationship with God and what we need to do to find our way into that kind of relationship.

Now there is a problem involved in that. We are all unique persons. God always relates to us in terms of our unique needs and possibilities. It is always a mistake to hope to have a religious experience just like someone else has had—or to insist that someone else should have a religious experience just like ours. Even so, there are some things we can say about what it is like to be in a life shaping relationship with God and what we can do to move into that kind of relationship.

One of the most helpful ways in which we can approach this subject is to study the eighth chapter of Paul's letter to the Romans. I have always believed that, in that chapter and the one just before it, the great theologian of the New Testament gave his personal witness to his own experience with God. He describes a dynamic and multifaceted interaction with a God who is alive and active. We can learn a lot by listening to his witness.

The starting point for Paul, and probably for the rest of us too, is to recognize a need in our lives.

Paul's story may not be typical because when his adventure in faith began, he was already a very religious man—a very, very religious man. But Paul came to realize that things were just not working in his life. At the end of the seventh chapter of his letter, he wrote, "So I find it to be a law that when I want to do what is good, evil lies close at hand. For I delight in the law of God in my inmost self, but I see in my members another law at war with the law in my mind, making me captive to the law of sin which dwells in my members. Wretched man that I am! Who will deliver me from this body of death." (Romans 7:21-24) I think it's fair to say that Paul started with an awareness of a need.

How are things working in your life? That may sound like the wrong question to ask. Lots of people today might say, "Just fine." Lots of people just do not feel any real need for religion. There was a time when most people were motivated to "get religion" by a fear of going to hell. Not so many people feel that motivation any more. And lots of people are already working some plan, often related to our culture's idea of success, that they think will bring fulfillment to their lives if they just keep on working at it long enough. That plan is their religion. They don't feel like they need any other. And, let's face it. Lots of people look at the lives of the religious people they know and don't see anything there that they need. That is sad.

But sometimes people eventually discover the futility of the plans they have made. Sometimes well ordered lives fall apart because of some flaw in the order or because life has pushed them into some situation with which they are not equipped to cope. And sometimes people take a good look at their lives—sometimes just as they are approaching what they thought would be the fulfillment of their hopes—and realize that they are not satisfied. Something is missing. An experience like that can make a person feel, as Paul felt, that things are just not working as they should.

Then, some people come to an openness to a new possibility in an entirely different way. They may have put together a pretty good life using all of the customary methods and materials, and then decide that they want something even better. They want life at its best.

Could there be something better for you? Ask yourself some questions. Do you love life—and yourself—and your fellow human beings—all of them? Are you making your life count for something good? Do you have a commitment to something bigger than yourself that gives your life purpose and meaning? Are you experiencing life in depth and finding joy in it? Do you have some strength of identity at the center of your life that makes you able to cope with the things you encounter in life? Do you experience life as an adventure? Have you come to terms with your own mortality and found peace? Dealing with questions like that may very well move a person to venture out into a new kind of life shaped by a relationship with God. How about you?

Paul evidently eventually came to feel good about his spiritual quest. The words that follow his cry of desperation are these: "Thanks be to God through Jesus Christ our Lord!" (Romans 7:25) In the meditations to follow, we will listen to Paul telling us about his adventure in faith. Some of the things that Paul says may not seem to relate to anything that could go on in your life. But then, some of it may. To say the least, it will show us an example of the kinds of things that can happen when a person ventures into a serious interaction with the living God. As a preview of what is to come, why don't you read through the eighth chapter of Paul's letter to the Romans? How about it? Are you up for an adventure?

Prayer: Lord, do you have something more for me than I have yet received?

Discovering a Possibility

Finding the way into a relationship with God must involve discovering a possibility. It must involve a belief that something big can happen, and that things can be different. Remember now, we are not talking about finding the way into some nice new avocation that we can attach to the edge of our lives, like taking up golf or joining a civic club. We are talking about finding the way into a set of new basic relationships that will reorganize your whole life from the center out. Lots of people avoid any such possibilities because of inertia or because of fear of the unknown or for many other reasons. They prefer not to even see that the possibilities are there. But those who have decided that there is a need in their lives, or that they want something more out of life than they have yet been able to reach, will go seeking the new possibility.

Let me share a personal story. Six years ago, my wife died. I spent a lot of time in grief. Our life together had been very good. In time, I decided that, since I was single, I would make the most of it. I did lots of interesting, life broadening things that I could not have done if I had not been single. My single life was good. But it was not what I wanted. Eventually, I found my way into relationship with a lady who had a similar experience. She too was open to a new possibility. We explored that possibility together and decided that it was what we both wanted. We knew that entering into that new relationship would make everything different. We chose the possibility. Now we are married. Life is different—and much better. Finding your way into relationship with God can be like that.

Paul, whom we have taken as our guide on this adventure, had to discover a new possibility. He had worked very hard at trying to put together a good life. He tried hard to live up to the high expectations of the Jewish religion as he knew it. But he just couldn't make it work. He felt the judgment of God resting on him because of his failures.

Then, one day, the very one whom he had regarded as the enemy of everything good, appeared to him and showed him a new vision of what God is like and of what life in relationship with God can be like. The risen Christ appeared to Paul and showed him that God is one who comes to us in love, accepts us as we are, forgives our wrongness, and works with us as a friend to help us become all that we can be. That opened an entirely new possibility for him. (Acts 9:1-22)

In his letter to the Romans, Paul summarized his discovery: "There is therefore now no condemnation for those who are in Christ Jesus. For the law of the spirit of life in Christ Jesus has set you free from the law of sin and death. For God has done what the law, weakened by the flesh could not do: by sending his own Son in the likeness of sinful flesh, and to deal with sin, he condemned sin in the flesh, so that the just requirement of the law might be fulfilled in us who walk not according to the flesh but according to the Spirit." (Romans 8:1-4) Paul decided to enter into the new possibility that had been shown to him—and it made everything different.

If we are to find our way into relationship with God, we will have to discover the new possibility that is there before us. For many of us, that will make it necessary to start one step further back than Paul did. We will have to rediscover the reality of God. God has always been there. We may even have believed that God is there. But many of us have gotten accustomed to living as if God is not there. A great poem and hymn that describes the ongoing drama of human history describes God as always standing there in the shadows, keeping watch above his own. ("Once to every man and nation." James Russell Lowell) It can mean a lot to us to know that God is there "keeping watch".

But the biblical tradition tells us that God is doing much more than just keeping watch. God is involved, in God's own way, in what is going on in human life and history. Can you visualize a greater reality there behind and within all of the other little realities with which we have to interact every day in life? We are talking now about an entirely new way of looking at life.

Let's go further. Can you visualize that greater reality coming to meet you in every new day, every new moment, every new experience of life? Can you visualize God being there in the situations of stress and threat and suffering as well as in the situations of peace and blessedness? Can you visualize all of your interactions with life as interactions with God?

Finally, can you visualize that one who comes to meet you in every experience of life being one who comes as Jesus came, accepting you, forgiving you, loving you, healing you when you need it, enabling you, teaching you the meaning of life and calling you to commit yourself to God's high purpose? Can you imagine going to meet each new experience of life asking what God may be trying to give you and what God may be requiring of you?

In the back of your mind, you may be thinking, "I am not sure that I can buy into that." It is not always obvious that a loving God is at work in every experience of our lives. Some of those experiences are pretty rough. To say that God is at work in those experiences is not to say that God wants them to happen as they do or that God makes them happen. (We will talk more about that later.) But it does mean that our relationship with God is worked out in our interactions with life. It does take some courage to believe that God is there and that God is there to do some loving work in your life. Paul was able to believe it. Lots of other people have been able to believe it. And for those who have been able to believe it, it changed everything.

Prayer: Lord, help me to know that you there.

Deciding Which Music You Will Dance To.

Once I had a funny experience that turned out to be surprisingly significant to me. I was driving down a city street with my car radio playing some popular music. When I stopped for a traffic light, I happened to notice some young people on an apartment balcony. They were dancing. And they appeared to be dancing to the music on my radio. Of course, the reason was obvious. They had their radio tuned to the same station to which I had mine tuned. As I thought about that, it occurred to me that there lots of different stations available to people who listen to radios at any time. Each plays its own kind of music. Every listener decides which station to tune in to, and what kind of music to listen to, and perhaps what kind of music to dance to.

Life in the world is a lot like that. At any given time, there are lots of different "voices" whispering—or mumbling—or speaking—or shouting in our ears. Each of them is trying to tell us what life is all about and who we are and how we ought to live our lives. Each is trying to get us to dance to their music. We have to decide whom we will listen to and who we will allow to tell us how to live our lives.

We know how powerful the influence of the peer group can be in the lives of young people. But different groups have powerful influences on us all. There are the always smiling people, or agencies, who want to sell us something. There are the advocates for various political philosophies who would like to brain wash us into their ways of thinking—and around election times their voices can sound like a constant drum roll. There are the "friends" or relatives who would like to get you to do things that are to their advantage, but not yours. Do you recognize those voices? Could you identify any other influences that are trying to get you to dance to their music?

Of course there are other voices too, voices that affirm your value as a person, voices that speak love to you in one way or another, voices that bring beauty and goodness into your life, voices that invite you to live life at its best.

The apostle Paul was aware of the different voices that are present in the world. He divided them into two categories. He associated those whose influence would be destructive with "the flesh". By that, he did not mean to say anything bad about our physical bodies or about sex or about any other physical aspect of God's good creation. Those things are gifts of God too. When Paul speaks of the things "of the flesh" he is talking about those forces that are at work in the world that are contrary to the life God wants for all of us. The destructive forces that were at work in the world in Paul's day were much more similar than you might think to the forces that are at work in our world today.

The influences that would lead us into the fullness of life that God wants for us are what Paul called the way of the Spirit. Paul could identify those influences that he associates with the Spirit among the many influences that come to bear upon our lives. (Look at Philippians 4:8-9 for a list of the influences that Paul associates with the way of the Spirit.) These are things that can be experienced in the everyday world. But Paul did not think of them as only human or natural things. He thought of them as things of the Spirit, that is, he thought of them as works of that aspect of God's own being that reaches out to relate to us in love. We are going to learn a lot about the work of the Spirit. It will be clear that Paul thought that the work of the living God can be experienced in some of the things that we encounter as we live in this world.

Paul tells us that we have to decide which of those voices we are going to listen to and which influences we are going to allow to shape our lives. He wrote: "For those who live according to the flesh set their minds on things of the flesh, but those who live according to the Spirit set their minds on things of the Spirit. To set the mind on things of the flesh is death, but to set the mind on things of the Spirit is life and peace. For this reason the mind that is set on the flesh is hostile to God;

it does not submit to God's law--indeed it cannot, and those who are in the flesh cannot please God." (Romans 8:5-8) You have to decide whose music you are going to dance to. And that is a very important decision.

Now, it is not as easy as you might think to decide which of the influences that come at us in life are "of the flesh" and which are "of the Spirit". It is not enough to just say that those influences that come in the name of religion are of the Spirit. Sadly, I have to say that some of the things I see being sold in the name of religion are just about as far as they can be from the kind of life that we should learn from Jesus Christ. And I have heard voices coming from secular sources—and even from other religions—that I believe came from God. It is not easy to tell whom we should listen to. The best thing to do is to ask which of the voices seem to be speaking for the way of love, that is, for a joyful commitment of life to life.

The decisions we make about whom we will allow to shape our lives really can make the difference between life and death. We will find that the flesh keeps telling us that we must measure up or be condemned. The Spirit will tell us that we are loved as we are and God can help us become all that we can be. The flesh keeps telling us that we have to conform to lots of different demands. The Spirit will set us free to live the life of love. Ultimately, the flesh will lead us to despair but the Spirit will lead us to assurance and to eternal hope. See, the difference really is the difference between life and death.

By now, we should see that we are going to have to make a decision about which music we are going to dance to.

Prayer: Lord, help me to hear your music and to know how to dance to it.

Getting In Touch

The Christian faith is not about living according to a set of rules or doctrines or rituals. Those things are helpful. But the Christian faith is primarily a matter of living in a relationship, a life shaping relationship with the living God. That aspect of the reality of God that reaches out to us to engage us in life shaping relationships is called the Spirit—or the Holy Spirit—or the Spirit of Christ—or the Spirit of the living God. Coming into a relationship with the living God can make all of the difference in the world.

Listen to what Paul said: "But you are not in the flesh; you are in the Spirit, since the Spirit of God dwells in you. Anyone who does not have the Spirit of Christ does not belong to him. But if Christ is in you, though the body is dead because of sin, the Spirit is life because of righteousness. If the Spirit of him who raised Jesus from the dead dwells in you, he who raised Christ from the dead will give life to your mortal bodies also through the Spirit that dwells in you." (Romans 8:9-11)

When Paul speaks of "righteousness", he is not talking about that arrogant attitude that we call "self-righteousness." He is talking about living in a right relationship with God. That is a relationship like the relationship that Jesus had with God the Father, a relationship of trust and love and faithful obedience. When we are in a right relationship with God, that relationship reshapes all of our other relationships, including our relationships with ourselves, with others, and with life as a whole. All of those relationships will be transformed into loving relationships. A right relationship with the living God is one that allows God to actually do important things in your life.

How do we get in touch with that great other? Some think that it can only happen through the sacraments of the church. Some think it happens only through an exciting emotional experience. For others, it is more of an intellectual thing. People are different. Getting in touch happens in different ways for different people. But whenever and however it happens, you should be open to it and "go with it".

I believe that it is important to allow the rituals and doctrines and teachings of our faith to teach us what to expect to find God doing in our lives and in our world. When we recognize God at work, we should open ourselves to what God is doing, receive it, respond to it, and commit ourselves to it. It is important for us to remember that the one in relationship with whom we are living our lives is someone who is alive beyond our imagination. Living a life shaped by an ongoing interaction with that one will bring us to life in new and exciting ways. There is no telling where our relationship with him will lead us. We can only know that it will never lead us any where that Jesus would not have had us go. The life of the Spirit will be a real adventure.

One of my favorite examples of a life shaped by a relationship with God is Tevia, the Papa in the musical, "Fiddler on the Roof". Tevia is a dairy man who milks his cows and delivers milk and other dairy products to his customers daily. He is also a man of prayer who carries on a running conversation with God about whatever is going on in his life at the time. I particularly like the scene in which Tevia'a horse has gone lame and he is having to pull his cart to deliver his dairy products. Eventually he gets so tired that he stops, looks into heaven, and says, "Lord, I am sick and tired of pulling this cart." He gazes upward for a while, then, bows his head reverently as if he had gotten an answer, turns around and starts pushing the cart. If you live in constant conversation with God, there is no telling where that conversation will lead you.

Prayer: Lord, it is exciting to know that you are reaching out to us. Help us to recognize what you are doing and to respond.

Claiming Freedom

There is an old movie about the Mafia that tells us that, if anyone was in need of help, he could go to the godfather and ask for a favor. The godfather would probably be glad to respond. But once the godfather has done you a favor, you are indebted to him. From then on, he can control your life. Is there any one or any thing that is playing the role of the godfather in your life? Are there any who keep reminding you of how much they have done for you and how much you owe them? Or are there any who keep telling you that they can do good things for you but, if you want what they can give you, you will have to do what they expect of you? (How about the materialistic culture that promises prosperity to those who do the right things?) Some of us feel pressured to live in certain ways just because we want people to like us.

Most of us don't realize how much our lives are shaped by the threats and promises that come to bear upon our lives. Often these things keep us from doing the things that that we really want to do and from being the people that we can and should become. Paul called that "being debtors to the flesh". He said it results in a kind of slavery—or bondage.

It is obvious that we are going to have to get free from that if we are going to become the kind of people God wants us to be. God wants us to be really alive, able to commit ourselves to great purposes, able to love. Somehow we are going to have to claim our freedom before we can respond to God's invitation.

A person who is in touch with God has a better chance of doing that than others. Those who claim that we are their debtors, or rather the whole gang of those who make claims on us, can seem awfully big, too big to resist. But if we are in touch with God, we will know that there is someone who is on our side that is bigger and more powerful than all of those. Do you remember that one of the ways in which the biblical witnesses described the saving work of God was to say that in Christ, God won a victory over all of the things that would hold us in bondage so that we can be free?

I once knew a young couple who were very "successful" very early in their lives. They were smart, attractive, and very capable. The man very quickly moved up into a position near the top of the organization by which he was employed. They had a big house in the right part of town, fine cars, and children in the best private schools. The only problem was that they were Christians—and the company was requiring the young man to implement some policies that he thought were not right. He talked with his employers about changing the policies but he could not persuade them. The couple thought and talked and prayed a lot about whether or not they could, in good conscience, live with the company policies. Finally, they decided that they could not. The young man did what he thought he had to do. He resigned from his position. They sold the big house and moved into a smaller house that they had owned as rental property. They put their children in public schools. They modified their life style. The young man took another job that paid only a third as much as he had been making and started over again at the bottom of the ladder.

I was so impressed by the couple's ability to claim their freedom that I told their story often. The responses I got were very interesting. Some understood and appreciated what the couple did. They leaned forward, smiling and nodding their heads as I spoke. But others recoiled visibly. They shook their heads and had a look of horror on their faces. It was as if they could not bear to hear how the story was going to end. These were people who could not claim their freedom and were threatened by the idea that they should.

God has put our lives into our hands and entrusted us with the freedom to make decisions that will shape them. God did that in the hope that we would use our freedom to choose the life for which we were created. (How many times have we said that in this series of meditations?) It can be costly to claim our freedom—but it can also be richly rewarding. God is at work in our lives to set us free for life in its fullness.

Paul wrote: "So then brothers and sisters, we are debtors not to the flesh to live according to the flesh—for if you live according to the flesh you will die; but if by the Spirit you put to death the deeds of the body, you will live. For all who are led by the spirit of God are children of God. For you did not receive the spirit of slavery to fall back into fear, but you have received the spirit of adoption." (Romans 8:12-15)

Prayer: Lord, give me the courage to claim my freedom.

Accepting Adoption

Some of the stories that inspire me most are the stories of adoptive parents who, instead of asking for the brightest and most beautiful of the babies available, ask for children who have been neglected or abused or are handicapped in some way. To do that is to take someone with very demanding needs into their homes and into the very center of their lives. It is to make a heroic commitment to love that will require a major portion of their life's energy for a major part of their lives. My own experience with parenting has taught me how demanding parenting can be under the best of circumstances. I can only imagine what those parents are up against.

But the adoption also makes some very special demands upon the children who are being adopted. It is very difficult for those children to move into their new set of family relationships. First, the children, whose harsh experiences may have taught them not to trust anyone or anything, have to find the courage to believe that the new parents can actually love them and to accept their new status as members of the family. Then they have to allow the the new relationships reshape their lives.

Jesus has shown us that we are the chosen children of God. We have been chosen in spite of our inadequacies and our wrongness and given a place in God's love. Almighty God has chosen to make a costly commitment to us. Can you believe that? Can you actually learn to know yourself as a loved child of God?

In our last reflection, we heard Paul urging us to claim our freedom and to take charge of our lives. He said "All who are led by the Spirit of God are children of God. For you did not receive a spirit of slavery to fall back into fear, but you have received a Spirit of adoption." (Romans 8:15) Paul goes on to say, "When we cry, 'Abba! Father!' It is that very Spirit bearing witness with our spirit that we are children of God … and joint heirs with Christ--if, in fact, we suffer with him so that we can also be glorified with him." (Romans 8:15-17)

Paul tells us that the Spirit of God, the active presence of God in our lives, is always trying to get through to us to help us know ourselves as children of God. God reaches out to speak that word of adoption to you through every experience in which your value is affirmed, every experience in which you know yourselves to be loved. And, if there are not enough of those experiences, the Spirit reaches out to us through the biblical witnesses to God's love for you and invites you to believe in spite of the harsh contradictions of life, that you are a beloved child of God.

Believing that should do two things for you. It should give you a sense of your own dignity and a sense of having a place to stand in the whole of reality. It invites you to love yourselves and to say "yes" to yourselves in spite of all of the experiences that say "no!" And, as we have said, it invites you to claim your freedom and to take charge of your lives.

The second thing that believing should do for you is to make you want to learn to live like a child of God. When we talk about claiming our freedom, we must know that there are some—many—who may choose to use freedom to become something other than what God has created us to be. There are many for whom the word "freedom" means permission to be irresponsible. Through Jesus, God has shown you what God wants you to be. You were created to be whole persons, liberated by faith, shaped by love, and committed to the high purpose of God for yourself and for the whole world. That is the heritage you share with Christ.

Like adoptive children, we need to get in touch with all of the experiences through which God is reaching out to us and allow them to shape our lives. That is not always easy. We have to learn that some of the influences that come to bear upon our lives come, not from God, but from somewhere else. We have to learn that some of the loving works God does in our lives are not always pleasant. There are corrections as well as affirmations, requirements as well as gifts. But if we will let them, the loving works of God can reshape our lives, just as the loving relationships of adoptive parents can reshape the lives of their children.

I once read an inspiring story about a pair of adoptive parents who took two very badly abused children into their home. The process of helping the children know themselves as beloved children took several years. But eventually the couple decided that it was time to take two more hurting children into their family. They worried for fear that the first children might feel jealous or threatened. But they did not. When the car from the agency brought the two new children, the first two adoptive children ran out to welcome them. The parents knew that the job would be easier this time. Of course, that is part of your role as an adopted child of God.

There is a passage in the first letter of John that sums this up beautifully. It says, "See what love the Father has given us that we should be called children of God; and that is what we are. ... Beloved, we are God's children now; what we will be has not yet been revealed. What we do know is this; when he is revealed, we will be like him, for we will see him as he is." (1John 3:1-2)

Prayer: Father!

Living Toward a New Age

Paul had a very interesting way of seeing everything that was going on around him, (and everything that is going on around us as well). He saw life as something that is being lived out between two ages.

On the one hand, he saw many things as parts of an old age that is passing away, an age in which things are winding down, falling apart, dying, an age characterized by futility and decay. He saw the shallow values of the pagan culture as parts of that age. He saw the political oppression of the Roman government as part of it. He even saw certain life stifling aspects of the religion in which he grew up as part of the age that is passing away. Paul believed that, even though the old age of superficiality and oppression often seemed to be dominant in many aspects of life, it is passing away.

On the other hand, Paul believed that a new age was dawning. He could see the evidence of its coming. It is an age of new life and vitality, an age in which things of lasting value like faith, hope and love are dominant, an age in which life is shaped by our interactions with the living God.

Paul taught that, even though we may have to live physically, at least for a while, under circumstances shaped by the age that is passing away, we can live spiritually in the new age that is dawning. Yes, we have to put up with the ways in which the old age is shaping life around us, and we sometimes have to "dance with it", but we don't have to be parts of it. We can learn to live in harmony with the new age that is coming into being and let it shape our lives. Yes, and we can let the new age make of us agents of renewal in the world.

In this, Paul has picked up on one of the great recurrent themes in the biblical literature. In the Hebrew Scriptures, during the worst days of the history of the Jewish people, the prophets told the people to expect God to do a new work to save his people. The prophet Isaiah spoke for God and said, "I am about to do a new thing; now it springs forth, do you not perceive it?" (Isaiah 43:19) Matthew, Mark, and Luke spoke of a new age that is dawning and called it "the Kingdom of God". (Mark 1:15) John called it eternal life. (John 3:16) And the book of Revelation leads us through chapter after chapter describing oppression, suffering, and conflict to a place where we can hear God saying "See, I am making all things new". (Revelation 21:5)

You have seen this, haven't you? Haven't you seen people who seemed to have all of the advantages living lives that had no real significance, or lives that are falling apart? Haven't you seen other people who were living under circumstances of poverty, or sickness, or debilitating old age but who were living life with a radiant spirit? And, in those times when everything around you in the world of society, politics, and economics seemed to be "going to hell in a hand basket", haven't you seen some people, groups and movements that seemed to have a better vision and who were working to make things better?

Paul described the situation in cosmic terms: "I consider that the sufferings of this present time are not worth comparing with the glory that is about to be revealed to us. For the creation waits in eager longing for the revealing of the children of God; for the creation was subjected to futility, not of its own will, but by the will of the one who subjected it, in hope that the creation itself will be set free from its bondage to decay and will obtain the freedom of the glory of children of God. We know that the whole creation has been groaning in labor pains until now; …"(Romans 8; 18-22) Isn't that a fascinating way of looking at reality around us, a creation groaning in labor pains to bring forth something new and exciting? Can you see it that way?

Then Paul brings us into the picture. Remember, Paul said that we have been given the status of children of God and the Spirit himself is working with us to help us learn to know ourselves as children of God and to learn how to live like children of God. (Romans: 8:12-17) Now Paul teaches us to see our becoming as participation in the birth of a new age for the whole creation. "We know that the whole creation has been groaning in labor pains until now; and not only the creation, but we ourselves who have the first fruits of the Spirit, groan inwardly while we wait for adoption, the redemption of our bodies. For in hope we were saved. Now hope that is seen is not hope. For who hopes for what is seen. But if we hope for what we do not see, we wait for it with patience. (Romans 8:18-25)

So we are given the status of children of God. But to accept that status is to commit ourselves to becoming becomers, people who are always growing and participating in the process by which a new creation is coming into being.

Let me share a personal reflection. What if you have been recently reminded that your own body is part of that which will either soon or eventually be passing away? That reminder can encourage us to get in touch with those things that are not passing away and to live the rest of life in terms of them. That will put us in touch with eternity. It can give us the assurance that the really important things to which we have committed ourselves in this life are not dependent upon us. They are parts of what God will ultimately bring to completion. And, when we learn to live in touch with eternity, we can come to believe that, in some ways that we may not be able to explain, we will be parts of the new age that will emerge. That is a matter of hoping for that which is unseen.

These are big ideas aren't they? We have to stretch our imaginations to catch the vision that Paul saw. But it is exciting, isn't it? Does it make you want to be part of what Paul is talking about? By the grace of God, you can.

Prayer: Lord, make me a part of what you are making new.

Letting God Fill the Gaps.

Have you ever found yourself in a situation in which you were invited to meet some other person whose greatness or intelligence or probable expectations were so overwhelming that you were reluctant to go to meet him or her? You found yourself saying, "I wouldn't know what to say." Or "I wouldn't know what to do." You might even have found yourself wanting to back away instead of moving into the relationship. If the possibility of any human relationship has ever made you feel unsure of yourself, it is understandable that the possibility of moving into a life shaping relationship with God could do the same thing.

If you are serious about venturing out into a new relationship with God and with life, your adventure will eventually take you to the boundaries of your own existence. God will call you to interactions that will require of you more than you have within yourself to give. There will be mysteries you can not understand. There will be important things that need doing that you will not be able to do. There will be relationships that will call for a love that you will not be able to give. You will find yourself reckoning with the inevitability of your own death. All of these things are implied in the statement, "We do not know how to pray as we ought." (Romans 8:26) When we are pushed up against the reality of our own limitedness, then many things will be made possible for us if we know that we are living in relationship with one who is not limited as we are.

Paul wrote, "Likewise the Spirit helps us in our weakness, for we do not know how to pray as we ought, but that very Spirit intercedes for us with sighs too deep for words. And God, who searches the heart, knows what is the mind of the Spirit, because the Spirit intercedes for the saints according to the will of God." (Romans 8:26-27)

This passage, that talks about one aspect of God's being talking with another aspect of God's being on our behalf, suggests the doctrine of the trinity that developed later in the history of Christian thought. What is so strange about that? Don't you sometimes talk things over with yourself? And God must be much more complex in his personhood than we are.

But let's back away from all of the theological complexities of the doctrine of the trinity and simply ask, "What is Paul trying to tell us here?" Paul is telling us that God understands our limitations and appreciates our intentions. God is always ready to fill in the gaps in our relationships with his own love. God is willing to work with us to complete the things that we will be called on to do. (We may be reminded of that passage in Hebrews 4:14-16 that says God understands because he has been there himself.)

It has meant a lot to me to know that God always continues to work beyond the places where my own abilities have limited out. That has been nowhere more precious than in my efforts at parenting. When my children were born, my wife and I knew that raising them up into whole persons would be one of the most important assignments we would ever receive. We committed ourselves to the task and gave it our best efforts. But eventually the time came when our children were approaching adulthood. We knew that there would soon be a limit to what we could do to shape their personhood. They were becoming separate persons. The task was not yet finished. It was an anxious time. Then a new understanding of God's grace was given to me. Grace is God's ability to do what we cannot do for ourselves. I came to realize that God would continue to work through other people and through other things going on in the lives of our children to complete the task. That assurance gave me the ability to give the task my best and then to entrust the rest to God.

That same assurance can be a valuable enabler every time we undertake any significant commitment. There are things to which we need to commit ourselves that we must know can never be accomplished within our life time. But the assurance that the Spirit intercedes for us can give us the courage to commit ourselves to the task with confidence.

The same assurance can give us something to hold on to as we approach the end of our physical existence. If we have learned to live out our limited existence trusting God who is not limited as we are, then we can approach the end of our physical existence with the same confidence.

Prayer: Thanks Lord. I need all of the help I can get.

Living In the Awesome Openness

One of the most troublesome beliefs that many religious people have is the belief that God is micromanaging the universe and intentionally causing everything that happens. It is not hard to get that idea from the Bible. Some of the Bible writers evidently thought that way. They would say things like: "The Lord hardened the heart of Pharaoh ..." (Exodus 9:12) or "Let your request be made known to God..." (Philippians 4:6) The Bible writers definitely believed that God does things. And you have heard me say that God works in life and in history to move us toward the fulfillment of God's purpose for us. But the Bible writers also believed that the decisions we make and the things we do make a difference. So, there must be some openness in the way things work that allows for many different possibilities.

Some people find some comfort in the idea that everything that happens is the will of God. But then, when something tragic happens or when grief strikes, those people often believe that God has failed them or that God is angry at them or that there must really not be a God after all.

If we understand God as Jesus has taught us to understand him, it will have to be obvious that lots of things happen that God doesn't want to happen. Wars happen. It is hard to imagine that a loving God wants wars to happen. Some people make messes of their lives. God doesn't want that to happen. Things like alcoholism and divorce and traffic accidents are parts of the drama of human life. But it is hard to imagine that God decided to make those things happen. People who believe that God sends natural disasters to punish the people who suffer from them paint a picture of God that is hard to love.

And yet, many people who have come through happenings like that can often tell of profound experiences they have had meeting God in the midst of those happenings. I once served for a while as pastor of a coastal community that had been devastated by a terrible hurricane. Many people told stories of life shaping experiences with God that happened in the aftermath of that disaster. But no one thought that God had sent the disaster to lead them into an encounter with God.

Paul helps us to get this issue into perspective. He says, "All things work together for good for those who love the Lord, who are called according to his purpose." (Romans 8:28) He did not say, "All things are good." Some things like traffic accidents and natural disasters and wars are definitely not good. And, by the way, some of the things that should have been good, like material prosperity and sexual pleasure, are sometimes made bad by people who abuse them. But God is present in our lives and in our world working toward the salvation of the world through whatever good and bad things are going on.

The trick is to recognize the saving works of God when they happen and to respond in ways that will allow them to make the difference they can make. Sometimes in the midst of some tragic situation, someone will reach out to you in a compassionate act and you will experience God's love through it. Sometimes being pushed up against your own limitations will teach you to trust God more and you will experience God's presence. Sometimes having to reckon with the results of your own bad decisions will force you to reckon with your need to make some changes and you will experience the judgment of God through that. Sometimes some great cause that needs to be served will call you to commitment and you will experience the calling of God through that. If you keep your eyes open you can see God working in all of these things and in others because the Bible has taught us that these are the kinds of things that God does. Just so, God can work in the awesome jumble of good and bad things that happen in your life and in your world to do good things. Remember that you are called to serve the purpose of God and keep asking, "What might God be doing in this situation?"

Paul says that God is always at work to help us become the people God wants us to be. He wrote: "For those whom he foreknew he also predestined to be conformed to the image of his Son, in order that he might be the first born within a large family." (Romans 8:29) In this case, the word "predestined" does not mean that God has assigned you a future that cannot be changed. It means that he has a purpose for you. God wants you to become a person who lives a life of faith and of love just as Jesus did.

Paul goes on to say that God is always working in all sorts of ways, some obvious and some not, to move you toward the fulfillment of God's purpose for you. "And those whom he predestined he also called; and those whom he called he also justified; and those whom he justified he also glorified." (Romans 8:30) God is always working in our lives and in our world to move us toward the very best future that anyone could hope for. It is just necessary for us to recognize what God is doing and to work with him.

Prayer: Lord, help me to understand what you are doing.

At the Last, a Victory

In many African American churches, the pastor's sermon will always end with a celebration. The body of the sermon may include revealing exposition of the scripture lesson and realist application to the problems of life in the world. But the pastor will always find in the message some good news to celebrate. As he moves toward the climax of the sermon, he will bring the proclamation to a crescendo that invites the congregation to celebrate with him. As he does this, the people may come to their feet and begin to clap and respond with "amen" and other verbal affirmations of what the pastor has said. They participate in the celebration. (Henry H. Mitchell tells about that in his book, *Celebration and Experience in Preaching.* Nashville, Abingdon Press, 1990) It seems that Paul had in mind ending his great witness to his faith in a similar way. After leading us through an amazingly complex and profound explanation of what it can mean to come into a personal relationship with God, he ends with a celebration of the one affirmation that underlies the whole witness. That is the affirmation that God loves us and that nothing at all can take that love away from us.

I think it is significant that Paul was not celebrating any of the things that so many people today hope that life—and religion—will bring to them. Those were not the things that Paul either expected or received.

Paul was not celebrating the achievement of social prominence or material prosperity. We have reason to believe that Paul had grown up in a family that had those advantages. But he had let them go. He wrote to his friends that he could either take those things or leave them. (Philippians 4:10-14) In fact, Paul wrote that while he was in prison.

Neither did Paul think that he had all of the answers to all of the big questions of life. He spent the next three chapters of his letter to the Romans wrestling with one of the biggest unanswered questions in his own theology: "What about the people who do not believe in Jesus Christ?" He was especially concerned about his own people, the Jews. Even though he was firmly convinced that Jesus Christ has shown us the way to life, he could not believe that all of the others were lost. Then he spent the rest of his letter trying to help people learn to live as Christians in a pagan world. Quite frankly, he said it is not always easy to know what to do.

Neither did Paul give us the impression that he "had it all together". The relationship with God that he described to us has lots of growing edges and incomplete tasks and deep mysteries in it. Paul was comfortable being honest about that.

And yet, all of that was put into perspective and made manageable by the sure knowledge that God loves us.

As I write this, I am reflecting on some visits I have just made to some old friends whom I went to see because I thought they might need a visit. One professional woman told me how her career was brought to an abrupt end by a harsh dismissal from her last position. She also told me about how she was caring for her husband who was a cancer patient. An older man shared with me the horrors he had experienced as a soldier during the Second World War. He was a paratrooper. He had participated in the invasion of Normandy. He had also participated in the liberation of one of the Nazi death camps. One older woman shared with me her grief about her failing health and about the necessity of giving up her home to move into a nursing facility. A man shared with me his hope that his doctor would finally find the cause of the illness that had just put him into the hospital for the third time. None of these were happy experiences. And yet, none of these people were being destroyed by their experiences—because they were people of faith. Even though it was not mentioned in any of the visits, I knew that all of these people were living out their experiences surrounded by the unfailing love of God—and they knew it. That is something to celebrate.

Now let's read again the triumphant words with which Paul ends his witness to his faith. See if you can feel—and share—the celebration.

"What then are we to say about these things? If God is for us, who is against us? He who did not withhold his own Son, but gave him up for all of us, will he not with him also give us everything else? Who will bring any charge against God's elect? It is God who justifies. Who is to condemn? It is Jesus Christ who died, yes who was raised, who is at the right hand of God, who indeed intercedes for us. Who will separate us from the love of Christ? Will hardship, or distress, or persecution, or famine, or nakedness, or peril, or sword. As it is written, 'For your sake we are being killed all the day long; we are accounted as sheep to be slaughtered.' No, in all these things we are more than conquerors through him who loved us. For I am convinced that neither death, nor life, nor angels, nor rulers, nor things present, nor things to come, nor powers, nor height, nor depth, nor anything else in all creation, will be able to separate us from the love of God in Christ Jesus our Lord." (Romans 8:31-39)

Prayer: Yes!

Random Reflections on Some Really Big Questions

Church?

Is Church necessary? Lots of people today have problems with Church. It seems that we hear more people talking about why they should not be part of the church than we hear talking about why they should. Of course, many are just making excuses for not bothering with something that might interfere with a selfish life style. They want to play golf on Sunday mornings. But, many people have been disappointed in their experiences with the church. Many can make long lists of the ways in which the institutional church as they know it has fallen short of being what God has called it to be. (I could make a long list too.) Now there is a whole generation that has grown up outside of the church, looking at the church from the outside, and knowing about it only the negative things they have heard other people say about it,. They don't know about the good things that the church does. (I could make an even longer list of those.) We hear many people explaining that they are "spiritual" but not "religious" or that they reverence Jesus but have no use for "organized religion."

In spite of all of that, the fact remains that, when a person becomes really involved in a life shaping interaction with God through Jesus Christ, that person will have a need to be part of a fellowship of people who share the faith and a compulsion to be involved in carrying on the work of Christ in the world.

Once you are caught up in the saving work of God, you will find yourself being incorporated into something bigger than yourself. One of the biggest mistakes that some American Christians make is the belief that a relationship with the God who saves can be an entirely private and personal thing. The Bible doesn't seem to know anything about a religion that can be an entirely personal and private thing. In the

Hebrew Scriptures, to be saved is to be a part of the community that God has saved. And the book of The Acts of the Apostles in the New Testament makes it clear that those who experience the saving work of God in Jesus Christ are incorporated into a unique community of faith through which God works to carry forward the work that God began in Jesus Christ.

Luke wrote the book of Acts as the second volume of a two volume history of the saving work of God. The first volume, The Gospel According to Luke, tells the story of that unique event in history that was the life and ministry of Jesus Christ. The second volume tells the story of work that God did through a very special fellowship of believers called "the church" or "the body of Christ".

Just as the story of the beginning of the ministry of Jesus began with the Spirit of God coming to Jesus at his baptism, so the story of the ministry of the church began with the coming of the Holy Spirit to the church on the day of Pentecost. (Acts 2) The new believers were drawn into a fellowship in which they shared with each other the love they had learned from God. Then, very soon, they were sent out into the world to do all of the things that Jesus did, to make God's saving work known to those who needed it and to be agents for change in a world that needed to be saved.

It should be obvious that the work of the church is an essential part of the saving work of God. Without the church, we would never have heard of the story of Jesus. The church alone, among all of the movements in human history, has been specifically commissioned to carry on the work of Jesus. Now the church is a multifaceted, world wide movement. It lives and works in many different forms. There are lots of ways of being part of the church. Anyone who is serious about the Christian faith will find some way of becoming part of the movement.

I can't help remembering an experience I had a number of years ago when I went with a group of church people to visit China. We were walking down a street in Shanghai on a Sunday morning on the way to attend worship at the second service of a newly reopened Christian church. The people coming from the first service smiled at us and nodded silent but cordial greetings to their visitors. Those greetings meant a lot to us because of what we had learned.

The country was just emerging from the era of radical Maoist Communism called the Cultural Revolution. During that period, the practice of religion was prohibited. All places of Christian, Jewish, Muslim, and Buddhist worship were closed and the property taken over by the state. Anyone caught practicing any form of religion was subjected to severe punishment. Christian ministers were subjected to harsh "reeducatioin". The church lived under conditions of persecution. Foreign visitors were prohibited. China was virtually cut off from the rest of the world. People who had been involved with the work of the Christian mission in China wondered what had become of the church. For a period of thirty years, there was no report. When national policy changed and allowed for a measure of religious freedom, the world learned that the church had continued to live under those harsh conditions. Christians met in secret in small groups in the homes of believers. It was too important to them for them to give it up. When the numbers were tabulated, it was found that the number of Christians in China had actually grown during the thirty years of persecution. The church which we were going to attend filled its one thousand seat sanctuary three times each Sunday. As we met the people coming from worship we thought about what they must have endured to remain faithful. We knew, better than we had known before, that once a person really knows Jesus Christ, his or her faith and participation in the fellowship of the faithful becomes one of the most important things in his or her life.

Prayer: Lord, help me to find my place in your church.

Prayer, Being Honest With God

When Jesus gave his sermon on the mount, he gave us guidance about many things. In the sixth chapter of Matthew's Gospel, we hear Jesus teaching us to avoid hypocrisy. He tells us that it is better simply to be honest with ourselves and with others about who we are. Then Jesus goes on to talk about prayer. That is something we all need to hear. Lots of people are bewildered by the subject of prayer. They say, "I don't know how to pray." A very wise person said we should simply pray as we are able. Don't worry about getting it right. Just do it. Just turn yourself toward God and open yourself to God and let the interaction happen as it will. We might expect that Jesus would say we should just be honest with God about all that is going on in our lives. He says, "But whenever you pray, go into your room and shut the door and pray to your Father who is in secret..." (Matthew 6:6)

Being honest with God may seem to us to be a very awkward thing to do. Prayers should end with an attitude of humble submission—but they don't always have to start that way. Some of the most profound prayers in the Bible might well have started with the prayer saying, "Lord, I've got a crow to pick with you!" Psalm 22 and the book of Job are examples. God can handle our honesty.

What would it be like to just be honest with God? Let's follow the agenda for prayer that Jesus gave us in the prayer that we call The Lord's prayer. (Matthew 6: 9-14)

The first item on the agenda is our relationship with God itself. We are told to pray, "Our Father in heaven, hallowed be your name." That suggests a relationship of trust and reverence. But what if that is not how you find yourself related to God at any particular time? What if something has happened in your life that is causing you to be angry at life and to be unable to trust? Your relationship with life is your relationship with God. You may not even be able to visualize God being there to hear. Wouldn't it be best to start by simply being honest with God about that and talking it over with him? When members of a family have grievances that cause tensions in their relationships, it is best for them to talk them out. Wouldn't that be the best way to approach a God who knows us and accepts us as we are and loves us? Talking those things over with God can probably eventually bring us to the place where we will be ready to call him "Father" and to reverence his name.

Then we may need to have a similar kind of conversation with God about our goals and our values, the things we want out of life. Some of us have some pretty well defined ideas about that. Some of us pray pretty selfish prayers, like a child writing a letter to Santa Clause telling what he or she wants for Christmas. But Jesus tells us that we should pray, "Your kingdom come, your will be done on earth as it is in heaven." Jesus tells us that we should learn to want for ourselves and for the whole world the things that God wants for us. Most of us know full well that the things God wants for us are the things that are best for us. But we may need some help in learning to want those things for ourselves and for our world. It could be helpful for us to have a really honest conversation with God about that.

We are invited to make our real needs known to God and to ask for the things that are important to us. "Give us this day our daily bread." When real love for self and for others is the motive for our prayer, we ought to simply make our requests known. If the requests are not healthy ones, we may recognize that in the process of asking. If they are, we can know that God wants for us what is best for us. We must know that our prayers will not always be answered as we hope they will be. But if they are prayers made in love, God wants to hear them. When someone we love is sick, it is only natural to pray for healing. We know that healing cannot always happen. But not to ask for it would be to be dishonest with God. God invites us to ask.

Then we need to be honest with God about the things of which we are not proud. "And forgive us our debts"—or is it trespasses? In fact, the word we are looking for is "sins", the things that we have done that do harm to ourselves and others and that separate us from God. We don't like to think about those things. We like most to try to shut them out of our minds and we certainly would not want to bring them up in a conversation with God. But we need to. God has promised to forgive our sins and to help us get free from the motivations and bondages that make us do the wrong things. But that process can only begin when we are open and honest with God about what needs fixing in our lives. When we experience God forgiving our sins, we will be more able to forgive others.

And "Lead us not into temptation" or "do not bring us to the time of trial, but rescue us from the evil one." This is a little confusing. It is not God that leads us into trouble. We find our way into that for ourselves. But we can ask God to go with us as we venture out into life and cope with the trials and temptations that are bound to meet us there. God is with us. If we can remind ourselves to trust God for guidance and enablement, we will be much more ready to cope with whatever we encounter.

There is no set format for a proper prayer. In fact, it might be said that there is no wrong way to do it. But the closer we can come to simply having an honest conversation with God, the better our chances will be for making prayer work.

Prayer Lord, teach me to pray.

Doing the Right Thing.

It is important for us to do the right things. The decisions we make and the things we do shape our lives and the lives of others whose lives touch ours, and ultimately the history of the human race.

But sometimes it is hard to know what is the right thing to do. You might think that just knowing the rules about what is right and what is wrong would be enough. But sometimes it is more complicated than that. Let me give you an example.

As Hurricane Katrina roared toward New Orleans, many people had to make decisions about what to do to survive the crisis. The city and the country were really unprepared. The results would be disastrous for many people. But many people and many communities organized themselves, more or less spontaneously, to do what they could do in the time of crisis.

One community in western Louisiana opened a public building as a shelter for refugees, even though they knew that many people in New Orleans had no way to evacuate. Many people who were able to evacuate crowded into the center. One deputy sheriff, who was also a part time minister, was on duty in uniform at the center. In the midst of the confusion, a woman approached him with the keys to a school buss in her hand. She asked, "Where should I go to turn this buss in?" The officer asked what she meant. He had a kind of a confusing conversation with her. No arrangements had been made to receive busses. Finally he got the picture. With the storm bearing down on the unprepared city, this woman had found a school buss standing idol. She had managed to get it started. She had filled it with poor people who had no way to escape from the storm. Then she had driven them to safety. The woman had stolen a school buss. The deputy knew perfectly well that it is against the law to steal a school bus. But he also knew that, under the circumstances, it was the right thing to do. When he finally got the picture, he laughed, accepted the keys and did not ask the woman's name.

During the Second World War, the whole world was in a crisis situation that made all of the traditional rules of morality relative. A whole new system of ethics emerged called existentialism. Even under more or less normal circumstances, life seems to have a way of backing us into situations in which we have to decide between alternatives that are all partially good and partially bad. Seldom do we get a chance to simply decide between right and wrong. And, in many of these situations, the worst thing we can do is to decide not to decide. Indecisiveness can often have tragic results. We will have to accept responsibility for those results.

So how should we go about deciding what is the right thing to do? Here are some questions to ask in the process of deciding.

First, you need to understand the situation in all of its dimensions. It is sometimes necessary to ask scientific and technical questions before you can see what really is right and wrong. You need to know something about biology to make a decision about stem cell research. You need to understand all of the dimensions of a patient's physical condition before you can make a decision about withdrawing life support. Questions about complex issues, like those having to do with homosexuality and abortion, have dimensions so bewildering that they leave us knowing that we really can't be sure what is the right thing to do. You need to understand as much as you can about what is going on in the world in order to responsibly cast a vote. What are the possibilities in the situation—and what might be the cost of each course of action. Responsible action needs to be informed action.

Then ask what the moral teachings of your faith and your cultural tradition teach. The Ten Commandments may sometimes have to be compromised, (as in the case of stealing a buss to rescue refugees), but for people in the Judeo-Christian religious heritage, they must always be taken seriously. And Christians must always ask, "What does love require?" love for self, love for God, love for all humankind.

Ask who you yourself are and what integrity requires of you. Can you take a course of action and still respect yourself. When crisis pushes you to make really difficult decisions, you may have to rely on the forgiving and healing love of God to make you able to recover after doing something that you feel just has to be done. When a compromise has to be made, call it what it is. Call it necessary but don't call it right.

Finally, ask about the results that would follow from all of the alternative courses of action before you. Will a decision move the situation—and the world we live in—toward a better future or toward a worse one? If a course of action seems to be good for you or for some person or group, ask still, "Will this course of action do damage to the moral structure of human society?" That is really the biggest question.

It is not always easy to know what is the right thing to do. But it is always the right thing to do to ask "What is the right thing to do?"

Prayer: Lord, stand by. I may need some help in deciding what is the right thing to do.

The Problem of Poverty

I remember my first exposure to the reality of poverty in the "third world". It hit me in the face like a certain well propelled boxing glove I once encountered, (the one that convinced me that I did not want to be a boxer). The exposure came while I was on a mission trip visiting Haiti, the poorest country in the western hemisphere. I had been there less than an hour. The buss that took us from the airport in Port Au Prince to our accommodations passed along a road from which we could see the beautiful Caribbean Sea to the right. But on the left we saw a vast hillside crowded with the tiny cinder block and sheet metal houses of the poor. There were thousands of them stretching from the sea up to the summit where the Catholic cathedral stood. The people were crowded in among them, cooking on charcoal fires, doing laundry, going about their tasks of every day life—or just standing around in groups that crowded the streets that dissected the slums. They stood around because there was nothing else to do. We were told that the houses were so small that members of large families had to take turns sleeping. (This was before the massive earthquake that brought destruction to so much of the city.)

During the week, we would learn about the effects of over population, deforestation, exploitation, political oppression, and a world economic system that works to make the advantaged people of the earth more prosperous and to reduce the disadvantaged to desperate poverty. I had heard about these things before. But on the way from the airport in Port Au Prince, I saw it. It was a reality. Eventually I was to see similar conditions in India and Brazil. It is part of what is going on in our world.

During my stay in Haiti, I came to admire the people who struggled to make life work under those circumstances. I admired them for being eager to work for two dollars a day when they could get jobs, even though they knew they might not get paid. I admired the local pastors, none of whom had been to seminary, but who served bravely , preaching the gospel, pastoring their people and also acting as community organizers and first aid workers. They turned their little church buildings into places of vital worship and also school rooms, clinics, and agricultural cooperatives that enabled the farmers to maximize the profit from their work. I met a person who has been one of the heroes of the faith for me. He was a little man, a leader in our church, who had also become a national leader in preparing the people for their first democratic elections. He continued his work until a night when he and his family narrowly escaped death at the hands of some of the enemies of freedom. They had to become a refugee. But most of all I admired the Haitian people who worked hard and managed creatively to try to survive under really oppressive circumstances.

There is a mythology that we often hear that says the advantaged people have their advantages because they work hard and are productive and do other things that cause them to deserve their advantages and the poor people are poor because they are either lazy or incompetent. In Haiti I learned that mythology is simply not true. The world's economic system works in a way that causes the disadvantaged people of the world to be pressed into poverty because of circumstances that are beyond their control. I became very aware that I am among the advantaged people of the world, not because of any virtue of my own—or of my country's. I am no better than those poor people in Haiti. Studies have shown that the world's economic system works in ways that result in the concentration of wealth in the hands of the most wealthy. The gap between the rich and the poor is widening. Now, even in the advantaged countries, the gap is widening so that the working people are becoming less advantaged even though they are becoming more productive.

There is something wrong with that picture. The book of Deuteronomy in the Bible is written as a collection of teachings that Moses gave to the people of Israel just before they went into their promised land. Those teachings describe the kind of life that God wanted his chosen people to live. People who take the Bible seriously can take those teachings as a description of the way in which God wants all nations to organize their lives. Two of those teachings are relevant to our world's economic system.

The first is the teaching that advantaged people should take their advantages as an occasion for gratitude and not for arrogance. Even though we have worked and been productive, our advantages are something that have been given to us. The book of Deuteronomy has Moses saying to the people, (When you have entered the Promised Land), "Take care that you do not forget the Lord your God, by failing to keep his commandment, his ordinances and his statutes which I am commanding you today. When you have eaten your fill and have built fine houses and live in them and when your herds and flocks multiply and your silver and gold multiply and all that you have is multiplied, then do not exalt yourself, forgetting the Lord your God who brought you out of the land of Egypt. ... Do not say to yourself, 'My power and the might of my hand has gotten me this wealth.' But remember the Lord your God who gives you the power to get wealth..." (Deuteronomy 8:11-17) The chapter goes on to remind the people that it was not because of their righteousness that God had chosen to bless them. Be grateful for all that has been given to you.

The second thing that the book of Deuteronomy has Moses saying is that a just economic system must be structured in a way that respects the rights and provides for the needs of the disadvantaged. "You shall not deprive a resident alien or an orphan of justice; you shall not take a widow's garment in pledge. Remember that you were a slave in the land of Egypt and the Lord redeemed you from there. Therefore I command you to do this." (Deuteronomy 24:17-21) It repeats this teaching several times. Then it goes on to establish a primitive welfare system by telling the farmers to leave some of their crops to be gleaned by the poor so that they will have a living. In the book of Leviticus, (chapter 25) there is a provision for every fiftieth year to be a year of Jubilee in which debts would be forgiven, slaves set free and land that had been forfeited in debts returned to its original owners. This was to prevent the accumulation of wealth in the hands of the elite and the impoverishment of the masses. Scholars tell us that custom was never practiced but the provision for it in the law represents a concern of the Lord.

What do these passages tell us about how things ought to be organized in human society? How could they be put into practice in our world's economy today? There are no easy answers. But these are important questions.

Prayer: Lord, teach me to care effectively.

The Hope of the World

In some of our earlier reflections, we spent a lot of time talking about the shape of the love that we can learn from the story of God's love in the first chapters of the Bible. We learned to think of love as a joyful commitment of life to life that begins with loving self and enlarges its circle until it includes God and everything that God loves. Love is wanting for those who are loved what is really good for them and being willing to do what we can to make that possible. The life of love is the truly good life for which we were created. We have also said that love is the hope of the world.

But is that realistic? In this world, where power politics and economics keep producing wars and oppression, is it realistic to talk about loving as a real option for the world? Was it even realistic in biblical days? The story of our first representatives in the biblical drama soon moves to a tragic chapter in which one brother murders the other in a fit of jealous rage. Things go downhill from there. Much of the saga of the Hebrew Scriptures is taken up with stories of personal conflicts, political intrigue, and destructive wars. You have to look hard to see that the story of God's love is being played out in that context—but it is there. Can love really represent the hope of the world?

Let me share one of my favorite stories. In 1986, I went with a group of church people on a mission trip to India. It was one of the most mind expanding experiences of my life. The high point of the whole experience was a visit with Mother Teresa of Calcutta, the nun who left the serenity of the convent to carry on a ministry of love among the destitute people who were left to die every night in the streets of India's cities. Her ministry had become a movement and she was eventually awarded a Nobel Prize.

Our group was ushered into a small room in Mother Teresa's compound to wait until she had finished her morning prayers. We sat waiting breathlessly. Through an open window, we could hear the hushed sounds of the young novices doing laundry in the court yard. We were expecting to meet a saint.

We had heard that mother Teresa had recently been asked to address a large gathering of heads of state who came to New York to celebrate the fortieth anniversary of the formation of the United Nations. Those were tense but hopeful days in the world's history. Ronald Reagan and Mikhail Gorbachev were just beginning the talks that would eventually end the cold war that had dominated world history for many years. We could only imagine how awesome that gathering must have been in its power and possibilities.

When Mother Teresa finally came into the room, she surprised us by popping into the room through a curtained door with a big smile on her face. She cheerfully shook everyone's hands like a cordial hostess. She saw that there were not enough chairs so she herself went out to get some more. Then she sat us down and asked "get acquainted" questions about us. Finally she invited us to ask any questions we had for her. Someone asked about her appearance before the United Nations. She smiled broadly, tossed her hands in the air like a happy grandmother and said: "Yes, I spoke to the United Nations and do you know what I told them? I told them to love one another."

We can just imagine what reaction that got from the powerful people gathered there. Some probably just disregarded it as the sort of thing you would expect from an elderly nun. Some might have thought wistfully, "I wish we could do that but in a world like this one, it is not possible." But perhaps there were some who saw in that message the one real hope for the world. Mother Teresa certainly intended for her message to be taken seriously.

Think seriously about that. To love means to want for yourself and your own people what is really best and to want the same for all other people as well. To love is to be committed to the well being of all people. Those ideas are not entirely strange. They show up in the rhetoric of many people and movements. But think about this: if every community and every race, and every industry and every business and every nation were really committed, not only to its own advantages, but to the well being of all people, would this world not be a different place?

Prayer: Lord, help me to hang my hopes for the world upon love.

The Possibility of Forgiving

Jesus said that we must be willing to forgive seventy seven times, (or seventy times seven in some translations), (Matthew 18:21-22) Sometimes it is important for us to be able to keep on trusting someone who has seriously disappointed us. Very often, the possibility of moving forward in personal or community life and relationships depends upon the possibility of forgiving. It is not easy to forgive. But faith can make it possible.

Now we are talking about something that is very complex, something that is not at all easy. It would be a big mistake to make the naïve assumption that it should be easy. But it is worth the pain and the risk involved in believing that it is possible.

This is one of those subjects that is best explained by using an example. I suppose that the best example would be a situation in which a marriage covenant has been violated by one partner who has either had an affair or has, in some other way, either neglected or damaged the basic relationship of mutual trust that is so necessary for the survival of a marriage.

When that happens, serious damage is done to some very important things. Damage is done to the self esteem and self confidence of the party who has been "sinned against". A marriage partner builds important aspects of his or her personhood upon the love promised in the marriage covenant. When that is violated, damage is bound to occur—often at levels of relatedness that are too deep to be easily surfaced or understood or worked through.

Damage is also done to a larger circle of relationships between family members or members of friendship groups. It is not unrealistic to say that damage is done to the larger structure of relatedness in all of human society. Systems of relationships upon which many things depend begin to fall apart. Things only get worse when the people involved start returning hurt for hurt.

And yet, sometimes a couple will decide that, even though a relationship has been seriously damaged, it is worth saving. (One thinks of a situation in which an automobile has been so seriously damaged in a wreck that the insurance company wants to call it a total loss but the owners decide that they want to save it.) When that happens, it is necessary to rebuild the basic relationship of trust. That will require someone—or someones—to give again the gift of trust to someone—or someones—who have at one time been untrustworthy.

That can only happen if there is a mutual commitment to rebuilding the relationship. Healthy love for self will keep a person from simply tolerating unfaithfulness. With a renewal of trust, there must be a renewal of expectations.

But where can a person whose primary relationship has been violated get the inner resources to enable him or her to take that risk? It can only come from having an even more primary relationship upon which the person can still depend. A person will need some solid place to stand while he or she is rebuilding a structure that is in shambles. A person whose basic sense of personhood is built upon the knowledge that there is a God who loves him or her may be able to take that risk. It will help if that knowledge of God's love has been channeled through other loving relationships. A person who has a sense of wholeness that is separate from the damaged relationship may be able to take the risk necessary to rebuild the relationship. That sounds awfully complex doesn't it? And yet many families have survived in just that way.

That same kind of action is needed in many other kinds of relationships. As this is being written, many people have lost confidence in their national and community governments. They feel that the government has failed them. And yet, the structures of government are necessary for life in a human community. It will be important for people who have been disappointed in their government to find the resources that will enable them to again give their government the gift of trust—and of expectation—yes, expectation—and to go on practicing their citizenship in it.

We have already said that many people have lost confidence in the church. Many people have been either hurt or disappointed in some ways that are serious enough to alienate them from the church. Of course, some are just looking for an excuse to sleep in on Sundays, but some have suffered real hurts and real disappointments that have resulted from the real failures of the church. (I know about that. In more than half a century of ordained ministry, I have suffered more of those hurts and disappointments than I care to list.) And yet, the church is important. To it has been entrusted the mission that is the hope of the world. That mission will not be accomplished by free floating individuals who describe themselves as being spiritual but not religious. It will be important for us to find the resources to again give to the church the gift of trust—yes, and of expectation.

But sometimes disappointment is even deeper and broader. Sometimes so many things seem to be falling apart in our lives and in our world that we may even question whether there is a God whom we can trust. When that happens, it is best to face that reality because we have a big decision to make. Jesus came telling us that there is indeed a God who loves us. In spite of all of the things in his own life that kept falling apart and letting him down, he kept on trusting. He kept on living in obedience to his God given purpose. And he kept on expecting God to be there. And God was. At least those who have lived out of the Christian faith through the ages believe that he was. It takes courage to believe that God is there in spite of all of the things in our experience that seem to deny it. But being able to believe makes lots of things possible. You are invited to dare to believe.

Prayer: Lord, I want to believe. Help me handle my unbelief.

Our Common Humanity

I want to share with you some thoughts that came to me a few months ago while I was sitting in the chapel of M. D. Anderson Cancer Center in Houston. That is probably the world's most advanced agency for the cure of cancer. You only have to walk around the hospital to notice the different races and nationalities represented in both the staff and the clientele. This is an agency committed to serving the whole world. The chapel was designed to serve this diverse constituency.

As I sat in the chapel, I could see that it had been designed to serve lots of different kinds of people. It has features that make it serve the worship needs of my own tradition. Pews are arranged in a circle around a plain altar with an altar rail where people can kneel. To one side of the altar is a pulpit where a speaker can stand. In a sculpture hanging over the altar, I could recognize a cross, the symbol of my own religious faith. But I could also recognize provisions for the practices of other religious groups too. Near the pulpit is a small cabinet which I knew would hold the elements of the Roman Catholic mass. There is also a small lamp suspended by a chain from the ceiling in which a flame flickered, a provision for Jewish worship. Near a large stained glass window facing east, I saw two small rugs, provision for Muslim prayers. In the foyer, I had seen pictures of Mahatma Gandhi, the Hindu holy man who had applied the teachings of Jesus for the shaping of the history of his country, India. All of this was very interesting to me.

I have long since moved past the bland liberalism that asserts that all religions are essentially the same. I have studied those other religions. I know that each of them represents a very particular way of understanding reality and a way of relating to it. They are different. My own religious faith, a particular form of Protestant Christianity, has its unique shape too. It is basically a belief that God loves us all and wants us all to love each other. (If you have read this far in my book, you have an idea what that is like.) Though I can understand and respect and appreciate all of those other religions, I am committed to my own. I am committed to letting it shape my life.

I have also moved past the naïve belief that "All religions are good." I have seen bad things done in the name of religion. As I noticed the Muslim prayer rugs, I could not avoid remembering that we were only a few days past the tenth anniversary of "9/11",the day on which some Muslims who had turned their religion into a religion of hate had committed one of the worst atrocities in recent history. As I looked at the flame flickering in the Jewish lamp, I remembered that I, who had never in my life held an anti-Semitic attitude, now have a grievance against the nation, Israel, because of the way they are treating the Palestinian Christians and Muslims in their country. I can think of atrocities committed in the name of all of the major religions, including Christianity. I recall that atrocities were committed in the name of the Christian faith during the partition of Yugoslavia. And I can think of things that are being done right now in the name of the Christian faith that make me ashamed. I believe that God will hold us all accountable for our acts of inhumanity.

And yet—and yet—as I sat in the chapel I was reminded of something that we all have in common. I had come to sit and try to come to terms with the news that my cancer had come back. I sat there hoping that the things I had always believed would become more real to me and be a resource for me. I felt a deep need to get in touch with God. I suppose that all of the people of all of the religions of the world share a common need, especially in the presence of their own limitedness and mortality, to find their way into relationship with that great other reality that stands over against us in life. Even Paul, who probably did more than any other person to define what it means to be a Christian, recognized that all people stand in some basic relationship of accountability before God. "For what can be known about God is plain to them, because God has shown it to them. Ever since the creation of the world, his eternal power and divine nature, invisible though they are, have been understood and seen through the things that he has made." (Romans 1:19-20)

When we stand alone and aware of our limitedness in the presence of the greater reality, in an awe and intimacy that transcends all form and doctrine, I believe that we must be aware that we are all parts of the same family. And I believe that we must learn to live together in a basic respect for and commitment to our common well-being.

Prayer: Lord, help me to see in every other person one who is essentially like me.

How great my delight.

What I thought were just hedges,

Bloomed with azaleas.

The Way

Jesus said, "I am the way, and the truth, and the life. No one comes to the Father except through me." (John 14:6) Some people think that means that, unless a person has made a profession of faith in Jesus Christ, he or she cannot go to heaven.

Lots of people find that a very troubling belief. They have friends who are Jewish or Buddhist or people who do not profess any religious faith but who are living conspicuously good lives. They cannot imagine them being excluded from the saving grace of God. Actually, to draw the circle that narrowly would exclude a huge percentage of the human race. That does seem to be incongruous with what we know about the God who comes seeking us in love. Let's take another look at that verse.

Jesus did not say he had come to call people to make a profession of faith in him. He said that he came to show us the way into a right relationship with God the Father. That is something much bigger and more basic. To find your way into a right relationship with God is to find your way into a right relationship with life and with yourself and with everything else. It is something that will reorganize everything in you life.

What is the shape of that relationship into which Jesus wants to lead us? It is a relationship that is based on a belief that the God who is God comes to meet us daily in love. That God calls us to relate to him and to life in a basic trust, a trust that the Bible calls faith, and in love, a love that is like the love with which God reaches out to us, a love that is a joyful commitment of life to life. To make a profession of faith in Christ should represent an intention to follow Jesus into that kind of relationship with God. It is a very good thing to make a profession of faith. But it is the faith and the love that are primary, not the formal profession.

If we feel a need to evaluate another person's life, and I am not sure we should feel any such need, then the question we should ask is, "Does that person live a loving life?" We may very well find some people who have never made a profession of faith living the kind of lives into which Jesus came to lead us. Sadly, we may find some people who are very proud that they have made a profession of faith and who are very confident that they are going to heaven after they die, who are living loveless lives. In fact, some may be found actually practicing hate in the name of the Christian faith. Everyone who sees that must know that there is something wrong with it.

It is true that there are some portions of the scripture that seem to emphasize the importance of being a professing Christian. Paul wrote, "…if you confess with your lips that Jesus is Lord and believe in your heart that God raised him from the grave, you will be saved" (Romans 10:9) But there are other portions of the scripture that affirm a more spacious acceptance of God. Only a few verses later, Paul wrote, "For there is no distinction between Jew and Greek; the same Lord is Lord of all and is generous to all who call upon him." (Romans 10:12)

Don't misunderstand what we are saying. It is simply not true that it doesn't matter what we believe and one way of life is as good as another. Some ways of life are all wrong. They are bad for those who live them and destructive to the world we live in. Jesus came to lead us into a very special kind of life and the way by which he leads us is demanding. A person who chooses to follow the way that Jesus came to show us will need to be constantly trying to live up to the example of love that God sets for us. And there is every reason to try to share our faith with others. We have something of great value to share. If it is the way of faith and love that we share, many people will find it attractive.

It is very clear that the people who wrote the New Testament were convinced that the way of a follower of Christ is the way to fullness of life. They had come to life in that way and they were very eager to share it. And it was clear that they thought of those who shared their faith as their family, the ones with whom they shared a special relationship.

Sometimes this commitment may seem to come across as exclusiveness. But when we find something said about who will not be saved, it most often has to do with the way a person lives, not with whether or not he or she has made a profession of faith..

All of that focuses on the shape that salvation takes in this life. The question remains, "Who will go to heaven after death?" We can safely leave that decision in the hands of God. When we go to meet that time, we should go trusting in the wonderful unmerited love of God that was shown to us in Jesus Christ, not in anything that we have either done or not done. We can entrust those whom we love to that same love of God, whether or not they have made a profession of faith.

Prayer: Lord, help me to follow the way that leads to life and help me to do what I can to lead others into that way too.

It Works If You Work It.

One of the most effective agents of redemption at work in our world is that organization that is called Alcoholics Anonymous. They are a fellowship of people who practice a twelve step spiritual program that is an effective application of the life shaping dynamic of the Christian faith to one particular problem. The people involved in A.A. take their work very seriously because they know that they have an urgent need and they believe the program can save their lives. One A.A. fellowship that I used to visit frequently had a very significant way of ending their meetings. They would stand together and repeat the Lord's Prayer. Then, in a volume just short of a shout, they would all say, "Keep a coming back. It works if you work it."

"It works if you work it." Every serious collection of authentic religious teachings needs to have that postscript attached to it. It is interesting that Jesus ended his sermon on the mount with a teaching that said, in effect, it only works if you work it.

The Sermon on the Mount is a collection of some of the most important teachings of Jesus. In them he tried to show us the shape of the life of one who would enter into the new possibility he called "The kingdom of heaven." Let's remember some of the things that he said.

He taught us to look for real happiness in unexpected places. "Blessed are the poor in spirit, for theirs is the kingdom of heaven." (Matthew 5:3-12)

He commissioned the faithful with their mission. "You are the salt of the earth." "You are the light of the world." (Matthew 5:13-16)

He taught us that the great religious teachings of the law and the prophets were intended to shape our inner lives and not just our outward motions. "You have heard that it was said to those of ancient times, 'You shall not murder.' But I say to you that if you are angry with a brother or sister, you will be liable to judgment..." (Matthew 5:17-43)

"He taught us that we should live out of an all inclusive love like God's love. "Love your enemies and pray for those who persecute you." (Matthew 5:43-48)

He said, "Beware of practicing your piety before others in order to be seen by them.." He taught us a form of prayer and of piety that would enable us to live in harmony with "Our Father in heaven..." (Matthew 6: 1-23)

He taught us to set our priorities right. "No man can serve two masters...You cannot serve God and wealth" (Matthew 6:24)

And he helped us to see that trusting God's providence can set us free for obedience to God's purpose. "Do not worry saying, 'What will we eat' or 'What will we drink?' or 'What will we wear?'"... "But strive first for the kingdom of God and his righteousness, and all of these things will be given to you as well." (Matthew 6:25-34)

He added several other teachings, the chief of which was this: "In everything do to others as you would have them do to you."Matthew 7:12)

He ended his teachings by saying: "Not everyone who says to me 'Lord, Lord' will enter the kingdom of heaven, but only the one who does the will of my Father in heaven." Then he told a story about two men who built houses. You know the story. One man built his house on the sand in the bottom of a seasonal river. When the rainy season floods came, they washed away the house. The other built his house on a solid foundation and the storms could not damage it. Jesus was not talking about building houses. He was talking about building lives. That is what all of his teachings are about. Only when these teachings are taken into the governing center of a person's being and allowed to shape his or her life from the inside out can they accomplish their purpose. (Matthew 7:21-27)

I have been sharing with you my reflections on religion and life. I hope you know that I have not intended to just be sharing interesting ideas with you. I hope you understand that I believe these things are insights into the vital truth that is shaping all reality. They are meant to lead you into a life shaping relationship with the living God who is at work to save in our lives and in our world. I sincerely believe that, if they are taken into your life, they will shape your life and lead you into the new possibility that God offers to us and to our whole world. I sincerely believe that, "It works if you work it."

Prayer: Lord, help me to know how to work it.

What If...?

What if it's not true? What if all of the things I have believed are not true? There is no scientific proof that they are true. I have accepted these beliefs in faith, knowing that I was choosing to believe in spite of all evidence to the contrary. What if it is not true? The question steals into our minds in the wakeful hours in the middle of the night, especially after you have gotten some news like, "The cancer is back." It would be foolish to pretend that does not happen. Some people say that we should never let ourselves ask that question. But, I think that, if I do not ask it when it is there to be asked, I will be basing my belief on a dishonesty.

The question is there. What if this world, with its processes so apparently intricately and miraculously put together, really is just an amazing accident that emerged in a vast universe full of infinite possibilities? What if these beliefs, that I have chosen to allow to shape my life, really are just the fabrications of some lonely souls, desperate to find meaning and hope in life? What if the realities I experience daily really are just a hodge-podge of random happenings and what if there is no great other there behind them all giving life and renewing life and loving me? What if, when I come to the end of this life, there really is nothing more?

Needless to say, I find the "what ifs?" harder to believe than the things that I do believe. But, if they were true—and all of the things I have believed are not—I would still be left with some treasures that I think cannot be denied.

I honestly believe that the way of love that Jesus taught, the way of mutual commitment to life, is the world's only hope of survival.

I believe that, not because I have made a prior commitment to my religious faith, but because I have taken an honest look at the history of the human race. All of the other currents in human history lead to destructive results. Only by moving to a commitment to the well being of all people can the world move toward peace with justice. That may seem like a pragmatic approach to religious faith, but to me it is convincing. It is convincing enough to win my active commitment.

I also believe that the values that Jesus taught are the way to fullness of life for persons. I have seen that in the lives of others and I have experienced it in my own life. When I reckon with the question, "What if this life is all there is?" I find myself coming up with a surprising answer. If this life is all there is, it will have been enough. I have lived long and experienced life deeply. I have reckoned with wrongness and limitation and tragedy and grief. But I have also experienced beauty and goodness and heroic nobility. I have loved and been loved. It has been good. I have experienced life as a wonderful gift.

And, because I have experienced life as a good gift, I dare to believe that this really is not all there is. I believe that there is a giver and that the giver is able to keep on giving beyond the end of my life. My experience of reality makes my faith make sense. I am not afraid to reckon with the "What ifs?". I know that I have chosen to believe in spite of all that seems to be to the contrary. And after reckoning with the questions that steal upon my mind in the midnight hours, I still believe.

Prayer: Lord, I have heard that there is a peace that surpasses understanding. Please Lord, give me that peace. (Philippians 4:4-9)

The Courage to Say "Come".

One afternoon, a number of years ago, my whole family and I got a life time supply of bull fights. We were on a family vacation in Mexico City and we wanted to witness a tradition that is well loved in a number of cultures. We chose a tour that included a visit to the bull ring. The experience did not make fans of us, but it gave us something to think about.

The event began with a lot of traditional ritual. The various players in the drama came into the ring, all dressed in their unique garbs. The matador, who was to be the protagonist in the drama, entered the ring with great fanfare, dressed in his "suit of lights". Finally, a huge black bull was released into the arena. The bull was an awesome, threatening presence. Several of the lesser players did their parts, mostly intended to torment the bull and make him mad. Then the matador steps into the center of the ring with his cape and faces the bull and shouted, "Venga", which means, "Come".

Now, I have to tell you that, under those same circumstances, I don't think I would have said that. I think I would have said, "Go.", "Go away." And if the bull did not take the suggestion, I think I would have said, "Okay, you stay right there and I will go away." But the matador said "come" and he stood his ground as the bull charged, gracefully stepping aside and managing his interactions with the bull with great bravery and dignity.

Later, I thought about what I had witnessed. I wondered about what it meant. I came to believe that , in the bull fight, the matador was representing the people who watched in a dramatization of something with which they could all identify. I have guessed that the bull represents everything that is dangerous and threatening that people have to deal with in life. It must also represent the threat of death. And the matador represents the people who watch in confronting all that the bull represents with great courage and dignity. If I am right in guessing what the bull fight is all about, I can understand why some people find it a meaningful thing to watch. And the drama begins when the matador says, "Come."

There is a place in the Bible where the word, "Come" is used in a similar way. It is in the next to last verse in the whole Bible, Revelation 22:20. The verse reads, "The one who testifies to these things says, 'Surely I am coming soon.' Amen. Come Lord Jesus." Now that will need some explaining.

The book of Revelation was written to encourage people who were living under conditions of oppression and persecution. It was written in highly symbolic images. It brings to the oppressed the promise that God is at work in life and in history to defeat oppression and to bring in a new era of peace and justice, an era in which life in the world will finally be the good life for which the world was created. The last two chapters of the book of Revelation give a highly symbolic description of what things will be like in that new era. But the book is realistic. It recognizes that these changes will not be brought about without great conflict and suffering. Most of the book is composed of symbolic descriptions of conflicts. The first readers would have recognized some of those conflicts as parts of their own past history. And they would have recognized that some of those symbolic stories represented trials and conflicts that are sill to come as God's purpose is worked out in the world. But having gotten human history into perspective and knowing that the saving work of God will be costly, the faithful say, "Come Lord Jesus."

There are lots of things about that message with we can identify. Anyone who has become involved in working for social or political change to wipe out injustice and oppression will know that such changes can only be accomplished through costly conflict. When we count the cost, many people decide that they would rather live with the status quo, even if that means enduring or tolerating injustice and oppression. But God is still at work in our world to wipe out injustice and oppression and God calls his faithful ones to participate in the costly conflict which will be needed to change the world. The faithful are still called to say, "Come Lord Jesus."

It is possible to interpret the book of Revelation more broadly as a reflection of the kind of change God wants to bring about in our personal lives. God wants to work in our lives to help us become the kinds of fully human people that God created us to be. The process of dying to an old way of life and being born again to a new way of life may not be accomplished without a certain amount of inner conflict and pain. But God comes to us in life wanting to lead us through those processes, however painful they might be, to fullness of life. Knowing that, the wise will still say, "Come Lord Jesus."

We have said again and again, God comes to meet us in all of our interactions with life and works through those experiences to lead us to fullness of life. Some of those experiences are obviously beautiful occasions for joy. But God also comes to meet us in those experiences that seem threatening to us, the challenging experiences like growing up, or looking for a job in a bad economy, the demanding experiences like family responsibility and citizenship, and the threatening experiences like grief and reckoning with our own mortality. We are often tempted to run away and hide from these experiences. But they are parts of life. And God comes to meet us in those experiences to enable us to live life. It takes great courage to go to meet those experiences and to live them out as interactions with God. But the promise of God invites us to say with regard to those experiences too, "Come Lord Jesus."

Dag Hammarskjold had a beautiful way of saying it: "Night is drawing nigh. For all that has been, thanks! To all that will be, Yes!" (*Markings*, New York, Alfred A. Knopf, 1964, p.89

Prayer: Give me the courage to say "Come".